D1649057

3/18/22

CASTLES
&
MOATS

CASTLES & MOATS

Insurance, Investment,
and Life Planning
Simply Explained

BRIAN CARDEN

Forefront
BOOKS

Securities and Advisory services offered through Madison Avenue Securities, LLC.

Member FINRA/SIPC, a registered investment advisor. Elite Insurance Solutions, LLC, and Madison Avenue Securities are not affiliated.

www.brokercheck.finra.org

DISCLOSURES

Investing involves risk, including the potential loss of principal. It is not possible to invest in an index. Any references to protection, safety, or lifetime income generally refer to fixed insurance products, never securities or investments. Insurance guarantees are backed by the financial strength and claims paying abilities of the issuing carrier.

This book is intended for informational purposes only. It is not intended to be used as the sole basis for financial decisions, nor should it be construed as advice designed to meet the particular needs of an individual's situation.

Madison Avenue Securities, LLC, and Brian Carden are not permitted to offer and no statement made during this presentation shall constitute tax or legal advice. Our firm is not affiliated with or endorsed by the US Government or any governmental agency.

The information and opinions contained herein provided by third parties have been obtained from sources believed to be reliable, but accuracy and completeness cannot be guaranteed by Madison Avenue Securities.

In honor of my mom, Ethel Carden, who gave me the gift of writing and sharing my words on paper and the memory of Dad. His wisdom, teaching, and love are written throughout these pages. As Dan Fogelberg said about his father in his song "Leader of the Band," I am his "living legacy."

TABLE OF CONTENTS

PART 1
BUILDING YOUR MOAT OF PROTECTION

PART 2
CREATING YOUR CASTLE OF WEALTH

APPENDIX

Acknowledgments

THERE ARE SO MANY PEOPLE WHO HAVE HELPED, guided, trained, and mentored me throughout my career, all of the successful days and not-so-successful days, that I could spend three pages on acknowledgments. Hopefully you know who you are, because I sure do!

This book would have stayed in a Word document forever without the help of the following people: Jonathan Merkh with Forefront Books, my golfing buddy and more importantly, my friend. He's the catalyst who told me to do this, and I can't thank him and his staff enough. To Allen Harris, my editor, who was very patient with me in the drafting, rewriting, correcting, and honing of this manuscript into something I'm quite proud of. And to Beth Tallent, my publicist, for her encouragement to complete this book and for her ongoing support in helping me help others.

Introduction

AFTER THIRTY-NINE YEARS IN THE INSURANCE AND investment business—and after gaining a lot of wisdom and experience in the financial world (often the hard way)—I've come to some realizations. The biggest one is that most Americans are totally confused about the who, what, when, where, why, and how of managing their finances, insurance needs, investments, and their other assets. Sometimes we feel like we don't know anything. Sometimes, we do. And, of course, there are the times when we *think* we understand something, but it turns out we don't. That's where we usually get into the most trouble. Like Mark Twain once said, "What gets us into trouble is not what we don't know. It's what we know for sure that just ain't so."

When I started in the financial and insurance industry in the early 1980s, there was little knowledge of the then-new Individual Retirement Accounts (IRA) or 401(k) plans. There were no "financial planners." You put $2,000 into an IRA or savings account, and they gave you a toaster! Yes, they actually did that. Mutual funds were just becoming available to the average person. Whole life insurance was still considered a valuable tool for protecting families and growing cash values. People saved money in three ways: savings accounts or Certificates of Deposit (CD) at the bank, payroll deduction for US Savings Bonds, or cash values in their life insurance policies. Only rich people bought stocks, and they could only buy them through a stockbroker. There were no college savings plans. Instead, we worked summer jobs or worked part-time while taking classes. People worked at the same company for forty years and then retired with a monthly pension check they would receive for the rest of their lives.

Things are a lot different today. You can find virtually every financial product, concept, or tool you could ever possibly imagine with a quick Google search. Hey, if it's on the Internet, it must be true, right? You can also get your fill of information from all the "financial entertainers" that are all over the airwaves, the media, podcasts, and the Internet. There is a ton of financial *information*...but virtually no *education* on how these financial tools work or how we should use them in our personal financial planning.

If you don't believe me, Google "financial planning" and you'll get at least 2.9 billion hits. "Mutual funds" returns 2.94 million hits. Again, lots of information but minimal education.

When I was a kid, Mom and Dad had insurance agents, stockbrokers, and bankers to go to with their financial questions. Believe it or not, these people *still* exist! Our immediate access of point-and-click, self-service options on the Internet has not replaced them—not yet anyway. And that's a good thing. We still need these professionals to help us reach our financial goals, to help guide us through the minefield of our personal finances . . . and to help us build our castles and dig our moats.

Why Me?

The title of this book—*Castles and Moats*—is a metaphor I've used for years, and it's the foundation for my belief system of how all of your insurance, investment, retirement, and life planning should work.

Simply put: if you're going to build a castle of financial wealth, you better build a moat of protection around it!

Just to be clear about why I'm writing this book, I assure you it's not because I like to hear myself talk, and it's not an item on this sixty-something-year-old guy's bucket list. I'm writing this because I've had basically the same handful of conversations over and over and over with friends and clients for nearly four decades. I have said that, in my purest form, I am a "financial psychologist." I have a business degree, but most of my work is emotionally based, helping people make good decisions with their finances.

One of my Realtor friends, who often overhears me on the phone when I'm working in his building, once asked, "Brian, don't take this the wrong way, but how many times a day do you have that exact conversation with prospects and clients?" We laughed . . . but I took it as a compliment that I said the same thing to so many people so frequently that he could recite it from memory.

So no, this book isn't an ego trip, nor is it a bucket list item. It's a tool to help my current and future clients, along with you, the reader, understand the method to my madness.

It's a resource that will answer your basic "castles and moats" questions and help you understand how to best use the financial products, professionals, and resources at your disposal.

Competing Voices

Imagine you are standing at the head of a large conference table, surrounded by all the people you have a professional relationship with. This could include:

- Financial advisor for investment management
- Insurance advisor for life and disability insurance
- Insurance agent for home, auto, landlord, and business coverages
- Real estate agent
- Mortgage broker
- Banker
- Human resources/corporate benefits representative
- CPA
- Attorney
- "Financial entertainer" (because you believe what they say)
- Your dad (because you've always trusted him)

You begin the meeting by saying, "I've invited all of you here today because I have a relationship with each of you and I want you to help me organize my finances and build a financial plan for me and my family."

Sounds simple enough. I mean, these are (mostly) professionals who spend much, if not all, of their time working with people's income and assets. Surely this meeting would go smoothly, right?

Probably not.

Most likely, there would be a lot of heated debates and arguments around the table, with each professional presenting his or her own opinion of what you should do. Even though you trust each of these people, everyone has a bias in their chosen field. The insurance guys think you should buy more of their products. The financial advisor wants more of your money to manage. The HR director thinks you should put as much as you can into your company-sponsored retirement accounts. They each have a vested interest in what you do, and they each are convinced that *their* way is the *right* way. But they can't *all* be right, can they?

In previous years, I taught a class I wrote called "Conducting Your Financial Symphony." It's a way of explaining this conference table scenario. Let's say each trusted professional plays a different instrument and the sound they make is them focusing on their individual instrument. Hopefully, you've been to a symphony before and know what I'm talking about.

So, what happens when the conductor takes the stage? Things get quiet and he or she leads everyone as a finely tuned orchestra making beautiful music together. Herein lies the question: Are you qualified to conduct your own financial symphony? If not you, then who?

If you see this as I do, then we're off to a great start toward optimizing this book.

I'm not professing to know everything. Actually, I'm learning more daily. However, I do know a lot about each of these options and, more importantly, I know how the professional financial planning game is played. Every financial services representative generally has a bias in favor of the type of work they do. If they work for an investment firm, then they're biased in favor of asset management. If they work for a life insurance company, then they're biased in favor of life insurance. They may call themselves "comprehensive financial planners," but they're not. Plus, if they work for one of the big household-name companies you are familiar with through advertising, branding, and funny commercials, they're almost certainly what's called a *captive agent*, meaning they can only sell that one brand-name company's products. Ever felt that sales pitch from someone who only has one product to sell? I've been on the other side of the table as that salesperson, so I totally understand how it feels!

In my career, I've been a captive agent on the property and casualty side and also on the financial and life insurance side. Today, though, I am an independent insurance and financial advisor. This means I have the freedom to represent multiple companies for multiple product lines. I get to shop around among all the different companies, products, and services to create a customized plan that perfectly meets my clients' needs. If I don't have it, I go find it!

Now, in my fifth decade in the business, I think this is the best option for the consumer, and it's how I'm going to present the material in this book. The good news is that you'll learn how to piece together the plan that's right for you; the bad news is that you can't get it all from a single stop-and-shop provider. You'll need to build a team. This way, you can prioritize, organize, strategize, and stress-test each financial decision to ensure the best outcome. Plus, you'll avoid wasting money on products that won't work well for you. By recapturing those lost dollars and redeploying them toward other, more fitting options, you'll have a much better result.

How to Use This Book

Even though I've titled this book *Castles and Moats*, I will address the moats first and the castles second. Why? Think about what a moat does: it's there to protect the castle from invasion or attack. So, when it comes to our finances, the moat represents the layer of protection we put around our finances *today*, and the castle represents our wealth-building *tomorrow*. That's how we'll approach the topics.

For starters, this isn't your typical sit-down-and-read-cover-to-cover book. Instead, it's designed to be my professional explainer's tool. Each chapter is its own module. If you are buying your first home, condominium, or investment property, there are specific chapters on those. If you're wondering if you have enough auto insurance (tip: you probably don't), there are a couple of chapters for that. Whatever need you're facing, I give you permission to skip around throughout the book, grab a pen, and please feel free to make a lot of notes in the margins and wherever I ask you to fill in some blanks regarding your personal plans. In each chapter, you'll find the same conversation I've had with my clients an infinite number of times as they've faced that need themselves.

Now, while you can (and should) skip around based on your needs, I did arrange the chapters in order of priority. If you're a young adult just starting out in life, consider chapter 1 your *Step 1*. Chapter 2 is *Step 2*, and so on. This gives you the invaluable opportunity to build your castle with intentionality from the ground up. For example, most people today immediately start contributing to their company 401(k) when they should be setting money aside for short-term needs, college debt payments, consumer debt reduction, and so on. There's nothing more frustrating than doing the right things at the wrong time only to realize the repercussions of your decisions after it's too late.

I should also say that my goal here is not to educate you on *every* aspect of these important topics. This isn't a graduate-level course on every insurance and investment product and strategy under the sun. Rather, my goal is to expose and break down the misinformation around the areas of insurance and wealth-building and arm you with the knowledge you need to make the right decisions for your family. I'm not interested in showing off how much I know. Unless you want to become a broker yourself, you don't need to know everything I know about this stuff. You just need to know what *you* need to know to make good decisions. So, I'll try to keep things short, sweet, and thoroughly unintimidating. I've actually given talks to groups entitled "Stuff That Makes Me Fun at Parties!"

The chapters will be fairly quick reads with no fluff. I could explain most of these individual topics in five minutes or less over coffee with a friend or client. I've learned that most people can absorb only so much info. Too little, and you might not understand or feel confident to make a decision.

Too much, and you might feel overwhelmed; so again, you don't do anything. I always aim for the middle—enough to educate and get my client to act, but not so much that their eyes glaze over.

That's the plan, and I'm ready to get started. I've always said I am a "professional explainer" of insurance and financial concepts. I guess it's time for me to live up to it!

PART 1

BUILDING YOUR MOAT OF PROTECTION

In business, I look for economic castles
protected by unbreachable moats.

—WARREN BUFFETT

CHAPTER 1

A CRASH COURSE ON AUTO INSURANCE

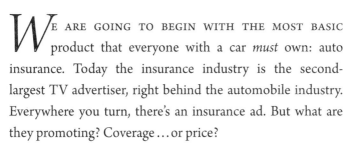

W E ARE GOING TO BEGIN WITH THE MOST BASIC product that everyone with a car *must* own: auto insurance. Today the insurance industry is the second-largest TV advertiser, right behind the automobile industry. Everywhere you turn, there's an insurance ad. But what are they promoting? Coverage ... or price?

Price, you betcha! It's all about cheap, cheap, and cheap. How do they provide you with cheap auto insurance? Simple—they cut your coverage to the bone.

Auto policies are *liability* policies in their purest form. They cover damage for which you are *liable*, meaning the accident was your fault or there's no other party who can or will take responsibility. In Tennessee, where I live, the bare minimum coverage to carry is $25,000 per person, $50,000 per occurrence, and $15,000 property damage, which is usually written as 25/50/15. That means, if you were to have an accident and had the minimum coverage, you would be protected for up to:

- $25,000 for *personal injury* expenses *per person* (example: the driver breaks his leg in the wreck)
- $50,000 for *personal injury* expenses *per occurrence* (meaning the insurance company will pay up to $50,000 total for the accident, no matter how many people were hurt or how expensive their medical bills are)
- $15,000 for *property damage* (meaning the insurance company will pay up to $15,000 to repair or replace the other person's car or whatever else you damaged)

When big, brand-name insurance companies advertise based on price, they're promoting a policy that represents a low out-of-pocket expense in premium costs for you. Take a minute to dig out your auto insurance policy or pull it up online to have it handy as you read through this section, as I'll discuss key factors you need to look for in your coverage.

Uninsured Motorist Coverage

The first key factor to look for in your car insurance policy is *uninsured motorist* coverage. Did you know uninsured motorist coverage is optional and you are not required to carry it? Many drivers don't know if they are protected against accidents with uninsured motorists. If you bought your insurance based on the low price of the advertised premiums, there's a chance you're not protected. This is a huge deal because there is a shockingly good chance that your next accident will be with an uninsured driver. I could never completely document this, but it's estimated that somewhere between 30 to 40 percent of Tennessee drivers have either no auto insurance in force or are carrying the minimum required limits mentioned. That means if you get into a wreck with one of these drivers, you'll be on the hook for your medical and property damage bills no matter who caused the accident.

It's almost a given that you've seen an endless stream of TV commercials and billboards advertising cheap insurance. What gets me are the commercials and billboards I usually see right beside them. Walking around downtown Nashville, every city bus I see driving by is covered with an advertisement for a lawyer that says something like, "You deserve to get paid!" or "Get cash for your accident!" How do these attorneys get this cash? Simple: they sue insurance companies. When that's not enough for their clients, the lawyers go after the defendants' assets and income. Think about it: If someone is hurt and angry enough to sue you for damages after an accident, do you think they care that you only have up to $25,000 in personal injury coverage per person and up to $15,000 in property damage coverage? No way. If someone is going to sue you, they want as much money as they can get—and the minimum state coverages won't cut it. You need a much bigger insurance program to protect you from that storm. Fortunately, there are policies for just such an occasion, which we'll talk about a bit later.

How Much Risk Are You Willing to Assume?

So, how much basic auto coverage *should* you have? Well, that's up to you as to how much risk you want to assume. You can carry the state minimums and *hope* you never find yourself in an accident caused by you or someone with minimum limits, or you can be more prudent and look to carry what I consider to be a reasonable bare minimum: $100,000 per person, $300,000 per occurrence, and $100,000 property damage (100/300/100) for *both* what you are liable for when the accident is your fault *and* if you're hit by an uninsured motorist.

A picture is worth a thousand words, right? Take a look at this snapshot from July 2008:

That *was* my car on the left. This is after the ambulance came and I was on the way to the hospital. The guy with his hands on his hips was my friend whom I called after the collision. I won't repeat the word he said when he got there.

The car on the right belonged to a young girl who was driving down this narrow road, texting on her phone, and not paying attention. No insurance, expired driver's license. She was two-thirds in my lane when I first saw her. I remember turning the wheel to about two o'clock, which is the only reason I wasn't hit head-on. No skid marks. No time to even think about the brakes.

Believe it or not, I walked away from that accident by the grace of God . . . and airbags. The whole thing might have lasted five or six seconds, but when I replay it in my mind, it goes on forever.

When a claims adjuster who looks at wrecked cars all day long asks, "How did you get out of that car, and how are you not hurt?" it makes you think. At the time I was carrying $250,000 personal injury coverage per occurrence and $500,000 total per accident for uninsured motorist coverage. That young girl could have completely ruined my life. It is within the realm of possibility that I could be totally paralyzed or bedridden today. Do you think she cared? Who really knows? Other than the police report, I didn't know any other information about her.

When talking to my clients about their insurance coverage, I always recommend the most they can buy at the best price they can get it, because I've seen firsthand how important it is. Benjamin Franklin said it best several hundred years ago: "Long after you've forgotten the price you've paid, you will remember the quality you bought."

Now, let's reverse this accident and say it was 100 percent my fault. But this time, the other driver is critically injured, and she consults the "get cash for your accident" attorney I mentioned earlier. How is that going to play out?

Let's say I'm carrying the $25,000 per person minimum state coverage. Do you think that will cover her out-of-pocket medical expenses, hospital stay, loss of wages, pain, suffering, and so on? Doubtful. After all, the advertisements say she "deserves" to get paid! So, how much is she going to sue me for? My guess is it'll be right around the magic number for lawsuits: $1 million. She'll probably win, too, if I'm as much to blame in this example as she was in the actual accident we had. So, we go to court and she gets a judgment for $1 million. How is this going to work out?

First there are the legal fees. Because the insurance company is only on the line for $25,000, their lawyer only represents me up to that amount. That means I need to get my own lawyer to represent me for the remaining $975,000. There's no telling how much I'd pay in legal fees in this situation, so we'll set them aside for now. But it'd be a lot.

Assume I make $100,000 a year as a widget salesman. I also just earned a one-time bonus (after tax) of $100,000. I have a house with equity, 401(k) plan at work, IRA rollover from my previous employer, and I have a permanent life insurance policy with cash value. Fortunately, retirement plan assets, such as IRAs, 401(k) plans, and company profit-sharing plan accounts, are creditor-protected. Because Tennessee is a homestead state (yours may not be), my personal residence is also protected. Because my life insurance policy has a beneficiary designation and is for the welfare of another person, my cash values are protected as well.

With all that in mind, here's how all this works out for me:

TOTAL JUDGMENT	$1,000,000
Insurance settlement	-25,000
Bonus	-100,000
IRA/401(k)	-0-
Home with equity	-0-
Cash value in life policy	-0-
Attorney fees	Indefinite
SUBTOTAL	**$875,000+**

If this were you, would you be in a position to write a $875,000 check plus legal fees? But wait! It gets worse!

In Tennessee, in this situation, cash assets and non-retirement assets (including investment real estate) are attachable in judgments. But here's the real kicker: after the initial amounts are collected, in the state of Tennessee, the court can garnish my wages annually in perpetuity until the debt is settled. Try accomplishing your financial dreams and goals with a high percentage of your income going out the window every month. Think that will put a dent in my future planning for virtually everything I want to do for myself and my family? You bet it will.

There is some good news, though. There are additional insurance coverages that are specifically designed to protect you in just such a situation. Even better, these options aren't even that expensive, especially considering the amount of protection they offer. We'll go through them next.

CHAPTER 2

OH, HAIL NO: UNDERSTANDING ADDITIONAL AUTO COVERAGES

*I*N THE PREVIOUS CHAPTER, WE UNPACKED THE BASIC liability coverage that's required for all drivers (although many still drive without it). Now, let's check out additional, optional coverages that can be just as important.

In its purest form, an auto policy is a liability policy. It protects against accidents and damages that you are liable for. The two main types of optional coverage you're probably somewhat familiar with are *comprehensive,* which is for "non-moving" issues (weather-related, theft, flood, hitting an animal), and *collision,* which is for accidents that happened while the car was moving (meaning you collided with another vehicle or structure). While liability coverage pays the bills for the *other* person when you're at fault in an accident, these two coverages are there to make sure *your* car gets fixed or replaced too.

The most common comprehensive claims are for things like:

- A tree falling on a car in the driveway
- Hail hitting the car while parked or while driving
- Windshield repair or replacement
- Theft
- Flood (which is covered by an auto policy, but not by homeowner's insurance)
- Hitting an animal in the road while your car is moving (a rare exception to the "non-moving" nature of comprehensive coverage).

What to Look for in Comprehensive Coverage

If you don't own a house with a garage, in my opinion, you must have comprehensive coverage. When a major hailstorm hit Middle Tennessee in March 2012, many cars were deemed "totaled" as the repair damage exceeded the actual cash value of the car. My nephew's car got caught in this hailstorm on campus at the University of Tennessee in Knoxville and—with no comprehensive coverage—he spent the next few years driving a car that looked like it had been sitting on a driving range! For this reason alone, I strongly encourage adding comprehensive coverage anytime a client asks for "liability only." After hearing me explain things, no one has ever turned it down.

As part of comprehensive coverage, I always recommend adding *full glass repair/replacement* coverage because it's a nice convenience to know your windshield can be fixed or replaced with zero out-of-pocket cost—especially when you're having to dodge flying rocks from potholes and work trucks on the highway. In addition, many newer cars and especially the high-end vehicles such as Mercedes, BMW, Jaguar, Tesla, Range Rover, and (believe it or not) Subaru require the dealership to completely replace the windshield when damaged because the technology of the car is connected to the windshield. Take a guess at what an S-Class Mercedes windshield costs? $500? $1,000? Try $2,400! I know because I've replaced countless numbers for clients, and all of them had full glass benefit, meaning zero out-of-pocket for the new windshield. Several of the big names in auto insurance talk about glass benefits, but other than covering the repair or replacement under comprehensive coverage subject to deductible, they don't offer this benefit.

When buying comprehensive car insurance, you should also make sure your insurance company will pay for original replacement parts from the manufacturer, known as OEM parts. Many insurance providers will only pay for off-brand parts when your car is being repaired, and that's often not the best solution for your vehicle. If you aren't sure if your insurance company will pay for OEM parts, ask your agent. If they don't offer it, consider going to another company or agency that can offer it.

Flood damage is a covered peril as well. Many of my friends and neighbors, not to mention my clients, suffered devastating losses in the great Nashville flood of 2010. Sadly, many homes did not have flood insurance, but their cars *were* covered if they had comprehensive auto insurance. Most were a total loss after sitting mostly underwater for a few days.

Finally, hitting an animal while your car is in motion technically qualifies as a comprehensive issue, even though you're moving. The reason is that you generally cannot avoid this situation, and the insurance industry has deemed it unfair to upcharge you for this surprise, which can cause a shocking amount of damage to a car.

What to Look for in Collision Coverage

Collision coverage does what it says: it covers property that you collide with. Backing into a mailbox or another car in a busy parking lot are considered collisions. This is great—often crucial—to have, but you have to be careful here. Just because the insurance company *can* foot the bill for a minor collision doesn't mean that's the best option for you. I recommend higher deductibles on this coverage because it helps prevent policyholders from making small claims, which almost always result in rate increases.

The average rate increase in Tennessee for a $1,000 claim payment is about 20 to 30 percent for three years. There are two separate issues at play here. If it's been a while since you made an insurance claim, you are possibly getting a "loss-free discount" for being claim-free that will go away once you make a claim. Then there's the surcharge—an increased annual premium you might receive at renewal for the actual claim itself. Oftentimes, it makes more financial sense in the long run to just pay for your damage out of pocket without actually making a claim against your policy.

I can illustrate this with a good example of a conversation I often have with newer clients who don't understand how their deductibles and coverages actually work.

CLIENT: "I want a lower deductible so I will pay less when I have a claim."

ME: "Let's talk about how to best use your insurance. Say you have a $500 deductible for collision. You back into your mailbox and cause $700 worth of damage. Then you call me, which is what I want you to do."

CLIENT: "Right. I'll want to file a claim so I will only have to pay my $500 deductible instead of $700 for the actual repair."

ME: "Yes, if you file this claim, you will only have to pay the $500 deductible. But when your policy renews, your premiums could go up around 20 to 30 percent. Are you sure you want to file this claim?"

CLIENT: "Well, why do I have insurance if I'm never going to use it? That's not fair!"

ME: "Your insurance is for the big stuff, not the little things. So, knowing what you now know, would you ever file a claim for such a small amount?"

CLIENT: "What do you recommend?"

ME: "Great question. The higher the deductible, the lower the premium. The lower the deductible, the higher the premium. (Read that again ... and maybe again.) Now that you know you would never file a small claim like that, why don't we raise your collision deductible to $1,000? That could save you a few hundred dollars per year, per car. Better yet, we could use that savings to increase other coverages in your policy so you're ultimately getting better coverage for the same money."

This is a typical conversation for me, and obviously I'll talk my clients out of filing a small claim to avoid a rate increase. Though annoying, it's those parking lot "love taps" that get you into trouble—especially if the other party files a claim on your insurance. You would be amazed how many people don't even know the claim was filed until they notice an increased premium at their policy renewal!

Other Auto Options

Medical payments coverage is designed to pay your or your passenger's medical expenses if you are injured in an accident, regardless of fault. This coverage is optional and I see many quotes where the agent or company representative cut corners to reduce the premium by either putting minimal coverage or, in many cases, none at all. At a minimum, you need at least $5,000.

Other optional coverages I've seen recently are *accident forgiveness* and *new(er) car replacement*. Many national companies are advertising these, and they can be helpful additions—if you qualify for them. Remember, just because it's advertised doesn't mean you qualify for it!

Accident forgiveness ties into the rate increases I was just talking about. With this additional option, when you have an at-fault accident in which damages are paid to yourself or another party, this benefit "forgives" (or avoids) that 30 percent rate increase . . . for the first accident but not the next one. To qualify, you must have a perfectly clean driving record for five years, meaning no tickets or accidents at all. See if your company offers this and if you qualify. It's a nice benefit for little annual expense. If you have teenage drivers in your household, this is a great benefit as with many young drivers, it's not a matter of *if* they will have an accident, but *when*.

New(er) car replacement is available to people who purchase, rather than lease, their vehicles and makes sure they get enough money to replace their car with the same or one-year-newer model year. This helps you avoid the pain and frustration of wrecking a new car but only receiving the depreciated value of the vehicle, which isn't enough to properly "replace" your nice car outright.

For example, I drive a 2018 vehicle that I bought new from the dealership. I have the new(er) car replacement option on my auto policy. In the event of a total loss, this benefit doesn't just give me the Kelley Blue Book value of the car I lost; it reimburses me enough money to purchase one model year newer, or in my case, a 2019. That would have worked pretty well if I had wrecked my 2018 car in 2020. I could have replaced it with a nicer, more recent model. However, if I'm still driving that 2018 car in 2026, a 2019 model year replacement won't be as much of a benefit. That's why it's good to stay on top of what coverages you're carrying year to year. However, given that your car takes the biggest depreciation hit in the first two years, new(er) car replacement can be a great feature for at least the first few years you own the car.

If you lease vehicles, you probably know this as "gap coverage," as it's generally required by the leasing company. Gap coverage is similar to new car replacement, and it is for situations where the vehicle is a total loss and the payment to the insured is less than the lease agreement calls for. It's designed to make the insured and the leasing company whole again.

I usually sell the value of new(er) car replacement to my clients with this short, totally true story. I had a client who bought his new car about a month after I bought mine in 2018. He called me one morning, and I could immediately tell something was wrong. Brand-new car, less than two weeks old, full of new buttons to press, switches to flip, and technology to play with. Short version: he wasn't paying attention on his drive home and smashed into a concrete culvert, totaling the car.

Fortunately, I had strongly encouraged him to add new(er) car replacement to his collision insurance, and the insurance company reimbursed him enough money to buy a brand-new model. It worked well for him in his situation. I still tell him he owes me big-time whenever I see him!

Car insurance companies are the number-two advertiser in the country. You cannot escape the commercials, banner

ads, and billboards. So, the next time you see an ad on TV—
now that you're armed with a little more knowledge—ask
yourself, "What are they trying to sell me: coverage or price?"
When I talk to new clients, I often ask them, "On a scale of
1–10, what is your IQ on insurance?" Would you believe I've
gotten negative numbers? So if you're one of those negative
number insurance buyers, do you really know what coverages
you need or don't need? See the advertising spin here?

Don't cheap out on your auto insurance or try to take this
on by yourself. Playing the price game could create a financial
nightmare if you're not careful. I promise, the few bucks you
save on inadequate coverage will cost you exponentially in the
long run.

What Brian Suggests

What My Current Policy Covers

100/300/100 or 250/500/100   _____

Deductibles

$500 Comprehensive   _____

Full glass benefit included   _____

$1,000 Collision   _____

Medical Payments $5,000 minimum   _____

Roadside assistance or towing   _____

Rental car coverage for 30 days   _____

Accident forgiveness benefit   _____

New(er) car replacement   _____

CHAPTER 3

PERSONAL LIABILITY POLICIES: AN UMBRELLA FOR THE STORMS OF LIFE

*I*N CHAPTER 1, I MENTIONED THAT IF SOMEONE IS HURT or mad enough to sue you over an accident in which you are at fault, they generally won't come after you for a small amount of money. Rarely will the person sue for an amount any less than what is covered under your auto policy's standard liability coverage. If they're going to the effort to sue you at all, they want to make sure it's worth their while. That means you need to be prepared for a potentially significant dollar amount against you. In the example I gave in chapter 1, we imagined I was sued for $1 million. My insurance paid the $25,000 they owed as part of my 25/50/15 auto coverage liability. I had another $100,000 in cash laying around that I put toward the judgment. That left me with $875,000 owed to the plaintiff. I don't know many people who are prepared to write a check that big. For most of us, a judgment like that would ruin our lives and steal our futures.

Good news: there's an insurance policy for just such an occasion. Better news: it is surprisingly inexpensive considering the enormous safety net it provides! I'm talking about personal liability policies, more commonly known as umbrella policies.

The industry focuses on both home and auto, and, of course, price, not coverage. So many people that I talk to have never been told about these types of insurance policies. These policies get the name *umbrella* because they are basically lawsuit protection and are designed to go on top of all your personal lines policies, including auto, home, landlord, boat, RV, jet ski, vacation home, and so on. Think of it like a shield that covers all your money and all your stuff, protecting it from lawsuits.

Umbrella policies are sold in blocks of $1 million increments, and they're extremely inexpensive considering what they actually protect. If you're price-centric, as most insurance agents and companies tend to be, this might be the first time you've ever heard of them. If you are protection-centric, like I am, hopefully you've heard of them.

Let's take the scenario from chapter 1 and play it out. First, I cannot have those minimum state limits of 25/50/15. Most of the insurance companies I represent require someone to have a minimum liability coverage of 250/500/100 to add an umbrella. Many direct-writing agents, like State Farm, Allstate, and Farmers, only require 100/300/100. Check with your agent to see what your provider requires.

So, now I have my 250/500/100 limits on my auto policy *plus* I have $1 million in personal liability (umbrella) in addition to that. Then, I have my at-fault accident coverage and, once again, I find myself in the courtroom facing a major lawsuit and an overzealous attorney. What happens now? Well, I'll probably lose the case if the accident was clearly my fault. However, this time, I'm covered!

TOTAL JUDGMENT	$1,000,000
Insurance settlement	-1,000,000
Bonus	I get to keep it!
IRA/401(k)	-0-
Home with equity	-0-
Cash value in life policy	-0-
Attorney fees	-0-

(insurance company is liable for the full amount)

SUBTOTAL   ZERO OUT OF POCKET

In addition, two additional key problems are solved. First, since the judgment is paid by my insurance company, my wages are not garnished, so I get to keep that amount that I had to pay in the original scenario. Secondly, remember when I had to hire my own attorneys for the amount that wasn't covered by insurance? In this scenario, the insurance company attorneys represented me at *their* expense. So my legal fees were a whopping $0 too.

What's the annual cost of a $1 million umbrella policy? Somewhere between $200 to $500 per year, depending on the client and their needs and what all it protects. Most agents can issue up to $5 million of coverage with no financial evidence. In this example, a $200 policy literally saved me $1 million! So, ask yourself, "Why hasn't my agent told me of these?"

Let's tweak the situation. Say the accident played out more like it did in real life, with that young, uninsured motorist slamming into me almost head-on. But this time, instead of walking away from it unscathed, we'll assume I suffered terrible, life-altering injuries. In the earlier scenario, I only had $250,000 coverage for uninsured motorist protection. But what if my needs total $1 million? Is that extra $750,000 coming out of my pocket? Did this young girl destroy my health *and* my financial future with her poor driving and negligence?

Maybe not.

This is on a company-by-company basis, and I cannot stress how important this benefit is for you and your family, but many of the insurance companies I represent will extend the umbrella coverage for my personal use in the event of an uninsured motorist claim for up to $1 million. So, by adding this additional benefit to my umbrella policy, I now have access to the needed $1 million for my own personal use. Consider it a "lump-sum disability" benefit in the event of a catastrophic event. Ask your agent about this if you don't already have it on your policy. It's too important an issue to ignore.

There are a handful of scenarios in which umbrellas should not be overlooked:

- You own a watercraft of some type, such as a boat or jet ski.
- You own rental properties with tenants.
- You have teenage drivers at home or away at college.
- You have regular savings and investment accounts (nonretirement).
- You have vested or nonvested stock options through your employer.
- You have inherited assets not in a trust.
- You make more than $75,000 per year in income.

- You have a title either in front of or after your name (Dr., JD, PhD, etc.).

If any of these is true for you, you need to talk to your agent today to make sure you're protected. It's just common sense: the best time to buy an umbrella is before the storm hits!

Liability Insurance Circa 1966: Real-Life Stuff from the Carden Archives

Before I wrap up this chapter on personal liability, let me pull a gem of a story from the Carden family archives that we wish had never happened. Like they say, "Facts tell but stories sell." So, let me see if I can sell you on the need for personal liability coverage by telling you how I personally almost ruined my family's lives.

Summer 1966. I'm almost seven years old, and my brother is five. We had been in our new home for less than a year. It was the house Mom and Dad had worked hard for, saved for, and finally built. We lived on a great street. It was about a half-mile long and was a dead end, meaning we could ride bikes, play all over the neighborhood, and feel completely safe. Besides, who wore helmets back then anyway? Mom's still there today, fifty-seven years later.

On the Fourth of July that year, the neighborhood had a big street party. Lots of people were there, and all the neighbors were setting off fireworks. My mom wouldn't let my brother and me have firecrackers or cherry bombs, though, because she knew we would probably blow ourselves up. So, she let us have sparklers instead. Sparklers *sound* safe, right?

But the thing is, sparklers are essentially just gunpowder glued onto a rusty wire. What could go wrong?

As it got dark, our neighbors began setting off all kinds of stuff—M-80s, Roman candles, cherry bombs, bottle rockets, and more. (Feeling nostalgic?) There my brother and I are, standing in the middle of all this just holding our sparklers. Excited by the explosions all around us, I turn to my little brother and yell, "Throw it, bro!" He does ... and it lands in the shirt pocket of our next-door neighbor's grandson. And it's still ... well ... *sparkling*.

So, he does what any young boy would do if his shirt suddenly caught fire: he freaks out. And, as he's running around trying to get the thing out of his pocket, he somehow manages to gouge his eye on the wire. Not only is he absolutely freaking out, but now he's jammed a rusty wire into his eyeball!

I'm terrified to think about how this would play out today, but here's what happened in 1966. The boy's parents took him to several doctors, and we stayed as close to the family as we could. One afternoon, the child's father came over with a piece of paper for my dad. He had an awkward look on his face as he said, "Gene, we really don't want to do this, but because of our son's medical bills, we've been advised we have to sue you." Then, he handed Dad the legal papers.

I often think of what my dad must have thought at that moment. Here's a young father of two who had just purchased his dream house after years of hard work and planning. How do you think he responded? How would *you* have responded?

Fortunately, this was 1966 and things weren't quite as cutthroat as they can be today. Mom and Dad went to Sunday School with a very nice man who was an attorney. Best-dressed man in the entire church! He worked with Dad's insurance company and our neighbor's attorneys, and together they settled everything fairly. The insurance company paid the damages, Dad never had to go to court, and most importantly, we remained friends with our neighbors throughout.

Personal liability insurance was key, even fifty-six years ago when the amounts were so much different. I'll bet Dad didn't even have $10,000 of personal liability. Heck, the whole house only cost $25,000!

Things would likely go much differently today. How big do you think the lawsuit would be if *your* child poked another kid's eye out with a flaming piece of wire? It'd be at least $1 million *guaranteed*. "You deserve to get paid," remember?

The bottom line is that you need good liability protection. You're only one mistake or accident away from potentially losing everything you have and everything you dream of having one day. Don't put your future at risk. Make the call today.

5 Reasons I Should Consider Purchasing an Umbrella Policy

- I own a home____auto____motorcycle____RV____ jet ski____rental home____
- My annual income is _____
- My children's ages are _____
- My total savings and investments not in a retirement account are $_____
- My estimated annual income for the next 10 years is $_____

CHAPTER 4

HOME SWEET HOMEOWNER'S INSURANCE

*I*F YOU LIVE SOMEWHERE AND HAVE SOME STUFF, YOU need some form of property insurance. I'm guessing that covers pretty much anyone reading this. When I say *property insurance,* I mean homeowners', condominium owners', renters', and landlord insurance. Whatever your living condition, there's a way to protect yourself, your home, and the property you keep there. As easy as it is to get an auto quote online, oftentimes it can be a challenge to get accurate property insurance quotes online. Using a real agent will benefit you as they can create a custom policy that includes not only what you think you should want but also additional coverages that you should consider. That's definitely a bonus for you in the long run.

Renters' Insurance

Let's start with something simple, yet something far too many people neglect: renters' insurance. Say you just moved to town, and you're renting until you buy your own home or condominium. You call me and ask about renters' insurance. I'll explain it this way.

Renters' insurance does three things. First, it covers your stuff in case of theft, fire, and other types of loss. If you live in an apartment, your chance of being burglarized is significantly higher than if you lived in a traditional single-family home, according to most estimates. And, if you're renting a house that belongs to someone else, their homeowner's policy will not cover your personal belongings. You've got to protect your own stuff.

Second, renters' insurance has a built-in liability coverage that protects your assets if, for example, someone gets hurt on the premises and comes after you in court. Believe it or not, the greatest cause of property lawsuits are dog bites. Even a Yorkie can hurt a child! And remember, people like to sue for large sums of money, so never get less than $500,000 in liability protection. (I'll explain more about this later in the chapter.)

Third, renters' insurance covers *loss of use*. A perfect example of this is the tornado that swept through my area in 2020. I had several clients whose apartment complexes got hit and were no longer livable. Their *loss of use* policies reimbursed them for the cost of getting new places to live while their building was being repaired or rebuilt.

These policies are insanely inexpensive—cheap enough that there is absolutely no excuse for any renter to not own one. In the event of a fire, theft, or catastrophic weather event, it's built to cover your personal property at *full replacement value*. That means you'll get enough to replace your five-year-old flat-screen TV that's now only worth $100 with a brand-new model at current retail price (after deductible).

Again, renters' insurance is far too important and far too inexpensive to skip. Do not tell me you cannot afford it. Besides, almost all home, auto, and umbrella insurance providers will give a bundle discount if you have all your policies with them. For the companies I work with, the discounts vary somewhere between 10 to 20 percent. The amount you would save on your auto insurance alone will probably pay for the renters' insurance, so always ask your agent for a bundle discount.

Condominium Insurance

Condominium insurance, also known as HO-6, can also be tricky for distinct reasons. Condo buildings have a homeowners association (HOA) made up of all the unit owners. The HOA is owned by the unit owners, and they have a master insurance policy for what are known as *common elements*. These are the exterior walls, roof, surrounding areas, parking or landscaping, swimming pool, tennis courts, clubhouse, and so on. The trickiness is in how they determine where *their* coverage stops and *yours* starts.

"Walls in coverage" was the norm in the past, but not so much anymore. That means anything attached to the walls inside your unit—from the drywall to the kitchen cabinets, fixtures in the bathroom, light fixtures on the ceiling, and the flooring—is considered part of and covered by the master HOA policy. In the event of a major event such as a fire, tornado, or lightning strike to the building, the master policy should cover those damages.

But (and there is always a but) what happens if you do something boneheaded like I did years ago and start a grease fire in your kitchen? Yes, I did that! Is that covered under the master policy? No! I'm on the hook for that.

The typical condominium owners' policy looks just like a renters' policy and usually includes coverage for your personal property and liability. However, as a rule, I will also add dwelling coverage, or Coverage A, to these policies, normally in the amount of 25 percent of the purchase price. So, a $400,000 condominium will have $100,000 of coverage to protect the owner in the event of something like my grease fire, or maybe if a unit owner upstairs rents his unit to a tenant whose negligence creates a water overflow issue that damages your unit. I've seen plenty of situations where the actual owner is nowhere to be found to accept responsibility. In those situations, your dwelling coverage would come into play to cover the damages to your unit. Water damage from an adjacent unit is one of the most common claims in multiple story buildings. This is a nightmare situation I am all too familiar with.

When I lived in a condo a decade ago, my upstairs neighbors flooded me *three times*. Once when a contractor started demolishing water pipes without turning off the water; again when one neighbor had a slow leak from his HVAC unit and just put a bucket under it to catch the water; and a third time when a hot water heater was installed improperly. I replaced hardwood floors three times in an eight-year period! The other parties paid for all of the claims as they were liable, but still it was a huge inconvenience. So, if you have an HO-6 policy, look to increase your dwelling coverage to at least 25 percent of the purchase price of the actual condo. It not only protects your personal home but also covers damages to another neighbor in the event it's your fault.

There is also an important, but rarely mentioned, definition in the HOA master deed. This is called "improvements and betterments." Here's an example of where you can think you have coverage, but you might not. Let's say that the condo complex was built in 1995. Needless to say, interior styles have changed since then. You buy the condo, and it has never been updated to current trends and your personal tastes. So you completely redo the kitchen cabinets, countertops, light fixtures, all of the bathrooms, replace all of the carpet, and upgrade the existing sheet vinyl flooring with new hardwood flooring. You spend a total of $50,000 improving the look and style of the unit.

Per the definition of "improvements and betterments," these improvements are generally not covered by the master HOA policy. When I add the Coverage A dwelling amount to the HO-6 policy, these improvements would be covered up to the amount added into the policy. Many agents overlook this coverage, and in specific situations where lenders do not require any coverage, this often gets overlooked. This is where it helps to have an insurance advisor who knows how to read the fine print. I have read countless numbers of these HOA documents…oftentimes alongside attorneys.

Homeowner's Insurance

Franklin D. Roosevelt once said, "Real estate cannot be lost or stolen, nor can it be carried away. Purchased with common sense, paid for in full, and managed with reasonable care, it is about the safest investment in the world." Purchasing a home will be one of the most significant events in your life, but homeowner's insurance can get a little tricky. Unlike auto insurance, it is challenging for the average consumer to do their own apples-to-apples comparison. The devil is in the details, and no two policies are exactly alike.

To begin with, a licensed agent is required to insure your homeowner's policy to its *full replacement value.* The industry standard is a replacement cost estimator provided by a company named Marshall & Swift/Boeckh. We input a variety of data on your new home and come up with the amount of insurance required to rebuild it in the current year. That is called Coverage A (dwelling) on your policy.

I've seen comparisons from five companies with five different replacement values, so who is right and who is wrong? Once again, it's the fine print that you need to be asking about. Let's say your new home has a $400,000 purchase price. However, the reconstruction cost is only $250,000. Why isn't the entire purchase price covered? Well, don't forget that the house itself isn't the only thing you originally purchased for

$400,000. That house is also sitting on a piece of land—land that you still own even if the house burns down. The location of that piece of land could account for a large amount of your initial home purchase. That's what they mean when they say the three most important factors in real estate are location, location, location. Because you still own the land the house was sitting on, you only need to insure the cost to rebuild the house on that same piece of real estate. That's why I insure the actual structure to $250,000 rather than $400,000. Make sense?

There are four types of homeowner's insurance coverages you should know, and a professional explainer like me can help guide you through the fine print:

- **Actual Cash Value**: replacement cost less property depreciation
- **Replacement Value**: what it takes to rebuild; current reconstruction costs
- **Extended Replacement Value**: a certain percentage or value *above* replacement value to rebuild
- **Guaranteed Replacement Value**: regardless of reconstruction costs, insurance company guarantees in writing to rebuild the home back to original status

When I'm reviewing any type of home insurance coverage with a client, I always use the phrase *stress test*. That is, I walk them through an example of how the different coverages work and what they would want in their policy going forward. I'll ask, "What is the worst thing that can happen to your home?" The answer is generally *fire*. Fire is a bad thing, but a house fire generally only affects you. How about wind? High winds, especially in the form of tornados, can knock down not just your house but the entire neighborhood.

My community recently experienced an EF4 tornado, which caused an estimated $1.6 billion in damage. Entire streets were destroyed, leaving only piles of wood and metal where rows of houses once stood. Let's use that situation as our stress test example.

Here's how the preceding definitions work in this kind of scenario:

Actual Cash Value might not be enough to repair your home because of depreciation. This means that even if your claim estimate is for $50,000, the depreciation value might be $10,000 less. I see this frequently with regard to wind/hail damage and roof replacement. Some companies are going this route to avoid putting brand-new roofs on homes where the shingles have exceeded their lifespan.

My client may expect to receive a new roof for "free," but in reality, they'll need to spend some money out of their own pocket because the value of the original roof has depreciated. Ask your agent if your roof has full replacement cost on your policy. However, in the event of an absolute total loss due to fire or wind (tornado, hurricane, etc.), the policy will pay out the full replacement value assuming you are going to build it back.

Replacement Value might be enough to rebuild your home in normal circumstances, but how about now? The entire community has to rebuild. What will it take in this situation, given the scarcity of building materials, labor, and the amount of devastation? Is $250,000 enough to rebuild your house if you're now competing against all your neighbors for builders' time and construction materials?

Extended Replacement Value is primarily for these situations. I normally recommend 150 to 200 percent of Coverage A depending on what company I'm recommending. In our example, that would be $250,000 × 150% = $375,000 total reconstruction costs. Again, the devil is in the details. Some of the household name-brand insurance companies only offer 110 to 125 percent, and you have to really dig to find those percentages. Every area has its unique natural disasters that displace many families without warning. In Tennessee, we have tornados. Southern coastal states have hurricanes. Out west, they have fires. All of these potential scenarios create a nightmare situation for you and your neighbors as you're all trying to rebuild at the same time.

Guaranteed Replacement Value was the standard many years ago, but given all the catastrophic scenarios we've had in the United States in the past twenty years, many companies have stopped offering it. However, there are a choice few that do. *Guaranteed* means just that: no matter the cost, the insurance company guarantees to rebuild your home. This is the platinum option if you can find it, so always ask if this is available.

The Different Coverages on the Standard Policy and How They Work Together

There are six basic coverages on a homeowner's policy. Here is a normal conversation I have with potential clients. For example, the quote I send them has the following coverages:

Coverage A	Dwelling	$250,000
	(replacement cost estimate)	
Coverage B	Other Structures	$25,000
Coverage C	Personal Property	$187,500
Coverage D	Loss of Use	Actual Loss
Coverage E	Personal Liability	$500,000
Coverage F	Medical Payments	$5,000
Deductible for all perils (including wind and hail)		$1,000
Extended replacement cost		150%

This is oftentimes a first-time homebuyer who is "shopping" for home insurance. Normally, their knowledge level is fairly low, so let's play out a scenario that will include everything above and how the coverages integrate. I ask them to open up the attached recommended homeowner's quote, and I will use a "worst case scenario" to show them how their home insurance will actually work.

So, let's assume that a tornado hits your neighborhood while you are at work. You come home . . . only to find out you no longer have one. It's been blown away by the tornado, along with several hundred other homes in your zip code. What happens next? (The normal answer is, "I don't know!")

First and foremost, call your agent and file a claim. They will be the voice of reason for you. That's their job. You should find out what your deductible is, if you don't already know. I always write policies in dollar amounts for a deductible ($1,000, $1,500, $2,500, and so on) rather than a percentage. I've seen some of the national carriers use a deductible as high as 5 percent of Coverage A, which would be $12,500 in this situation. Also, you should look to see if you have a separate deductible for wind and hail. Be sure you read the fine print of what you are buying.

The first policy provision you will initiate is Coverage D, Loss of Use. You can't live in your home, so you need a place to live while your home is being rebuilt, repaired, etc. Remember, all your neighbors are in the same situation, so expediency and patience are required on your part. Some companies put a dollar amount, some put actual loss. Again, read the fine print.

The second provision you will use is Coverage C, Personal Property. Personal property is almost always covered at full replacement. I talked about this earlier. When you actually "replace" it, the insurance company will reimburse you in full for the new item (subject to deductible, of course).

Let's say someone was working in your home when the tornado hit, and they fell and injured themselves. Coverage F (Medical Payments) gives them $5,000 to get checked out and pay for their out-of-pocket expenses.

So, we have a pretty disastrous scenario here. You've seen the devastation of tornados on the news, right? Everyone is trying to get their homes rebuilt and repaired on an ASAP basis. What if the cost of labor and building materials goes up substantially because of the laws of supply and demand? What if it costs $325,000 to rebuild your home and Coverage A says $250,000? Do we have a problem? (Loaded question.) Look at the line that says "Extended Replacement Cost = 150 percent." That means that you will have 150 percent of $250,000 (or, $375,000) available to rebuild your home. Are you okay with this? The answer is almost always *yes*!

Coverage B is Other Structures, so if you have a fence, gazebo, pool, detached garage, and so on, that is what this policy covers. The amount of coverage should accommodate what is on your property.

So, after your $1,000 deductible, we have found you a place to live, your stuff is going to be replaced, we have sufficient dollars available to rebuild your home, and, if anyone got hurt, you had money available for their care.

Optional Coverages Any Homeowner or Renter Should Consider

Now, let's look at the optional coverages you should consider, which are:

Scheduled Personal Property Insurance

If it's of value, it can be added to your home policy by "scheduling" it. The fundamental reason I always recommend this is that it is documented proof you owned the items. In the old days, Grandmother would insure her furs, silver service set, china, and, of course, her jewelry. I've scheduled vintage Pyrex bowls before, as they are apparently valuable. Who knew? If you've got valuable art on your walls; if you've got a diamond engagement ring; if you have a gun collection—whatever items of particular value you might own, have them appraised, send the documentation to your agent, and schedule them on your policy, whether you're a renter or homeowner. These items will be insured for full appraised value and for all perils.

Would you believe I have a client with several bottles of Pappy Van Winkle bourbon scheduled on his homeowner's policy? This is one of the most treasured bourbons made, and a single bottle can go for thousands of dollars. He got married a few years back, and for his bachelor party, he opened a bottle with his groomsmen. Oh, yes, he did call me the next day to take it off of his policy.

If you have a lot of jewelry worth several thousand dollars, ask about *blanket coverage*, where you increase the limits of jewelry on the policy. Most policies will have specific limits on certain types of personal property. A good example is someone that has a workshop and owns a lot of tools; either make sure that there isn't a limit in the policy on the value of tools or raise that particular limit to meet your needs.

Because I live in Music City, many of my clients schedule their musical instruments on their insurance policies. One of my favorite clients called me one day. He said he needed to add something he had just purchased to his insurance policy. I asked what it was, and he said, "I just left the Gibson Custom Shop and picked up my dream guitar!" I asked where the guitar was, and he said his back seat. Then I asked where he was going, and he said, "To a gig in Alabama!"

I had to tell him, "If you're using it in your profession as a musician, performer, songwriter, and so on, it's professional equipment and the musician's union should cover it. When you retire, I will add it to your homeowner's policy." I also told him that if he had a vintage instrument that rarely leaves his home or home studio, there was a possibility I could cover that as scheduled personal property.

I have played acoustic guitar since I was a teenager. I play for the love of it, not to perform or to make money doing it. I've got a few pretty nice acoustic guitars. Since I do not make a living with them, each of them is scheduled on my homeowner's policy at their full retail value.

One thing to remember: *you cannot insure sentimentality.* An item might have huge emotional value to you, such as your grandma's handmade quilts, but little actual value. In the event of a loss, it could be virtually impossible to find a replacement for them. It can be frustrating as there are just some things that insurance cannot cover.

Water Backup and Sewer/Sump Overflow

This is an optional coverage for the standard homeowner's and condominium policies, and it should be added on every policy. However, this coverage is often overlooked by those who buy their policy without the advice of a professional, or perhaps with a professional who shortcuts that coverage for price. Think about it. If sewage water goes backwards into the home because of backed-up drains or failed sump pumps, it's 100 percent nasty! How much will it cost to replace the flooring and any damaged personal property? For what it does, don't shortcut this coverage. I always add at least $10,000 of coverage to every policy I write.

Earthquake and Sinkhole

These are optional coverages that are available to you. Sinkhole coverage is just that: coverage for your dwelling if an area of land opens up and falls into the earth. Ever hear about the Corvette Museum sinkhole? The ground literally opened up in the middle of the Bowling Green, Kentucky, attraction in 2014, swallowing eight classic cars right off the showroom floor! The museum was sitting on miles and miles of underground caves, and one day the caves got hungry.

I have a good friend who lives close to the Tennessee River in Knoxville, and a sinkhole developed in her neighbor's yard. She didn't have sinkhole coverage and now she's got a preexisting condition. Here in Middle Tennessee, we're sitting on a huge sheet of limestone. I've got at least ten areas in my yard where rock is exposed, so I think I'm okay. When in doubt, ask your neighbors, ask your Realtor, and ask people who know the neighborhood and see what they say. If you feel you need to add it, just call your agent and they can do it.

Earthquake is an available coverage in most states. Talk to your Realtor and insurance advisor if it might be a coverage to add.

CHAPTER 5

LANDLORD POLICIES: PROTECTING HOMES YOU DON'T LIVE IN

*I*N THE PREVIOUS CHAPTER, I BROKE DOWN THE different types of coverage values for property owners, focusing primarily on one's personal residence. But what about property you own that you don't personally live in?

Investment real estate, when managed properly and effectively, can be a wonderful source of retirement income. With the decline of company pension plans, investment real estate can be your equivalent of that monthly pension check your parents and grandparents got. It also gives you the three key aspects of an investable asset:

- **Growth** through market appreciation
- **Income** through monthly rent
- **Tax advantages** through deductible mortgage interest, depreciation, and a whole lot more[1]

We'll talk more about the income and investment side of rental real estate later, when we discuss different *castle* strategies. For now, let's focus on the insurance implications around rental real estate.

Insuring Long-Term Rentals

Many people think their *landlord policy*—also known as a *dwelling fire policy*—should be close to the same price and coverage as their homeowner's policy, but they are looked at by the insurance companies as two totally separate risks. Nowadays, not all companies will write a stand-alone landlord policy. In addition, there are many companies that require that a rental property owner must also have their personal home, auto, and umbrella policies with the same insurance company that issues their landlord policy.

However, if an insurance company does write a stand-alone policy, it will most likely be written on an *Actual Cash Value* (ACV) basis. This means that the value the policy states will be subject to a depreciation value before it is paid out. For example, you may file a claim for $10,000 with a $1,000 deductible, but your policy has a 20 percent depreciation value. This means you'd actually receive only $8,000 (minus the $1,000 deductible), leaving you with $7,000 in cash. The *policy declaration page* may say the house is insured to replacement value, but the *policy language* includes that depreciation value. Look there to find it, or ask your agent what yours is.

The better alternative for most landlords is *Full Replacement Value* policies. These cost a little more, but to me it's well worth the additional cost. The benefit of full replacement is exactly that. A $50,000 claim will be paid in full to the insured (less deductible). A little more cost but a lot more benefit. Because insurance is so price-driven, I have to work hard to educate my clients on what they're buying. Most of the time, it's not an apples-to-apples comparison.

You can also include the *Extended Replacement Cost* option I mentioned in chapter 4. A few companies will offer this, but not all. Additional benefits mean additional cost, but you get so much more for your money—sometimes up to 125 percent coverage. Much better than the 80 percent ACV coverage we looked at earlier. Which would you rather have: 80 percent protection or 125 percent protection? If you're looking for *cheap*, you'll settle for the 80 percent ACV. If you want the best you can get, you'll go with the more expensive *Extended Replacement Cost* policy.

Insuring Short-Term Rentals

Short-term rentals, like Airbnb and VRBO, have hit the scene in a major way in recent years, and it's taken the insurance companies a while to catch up. I'll start by saying this as clearly as I can: if you are running short-term rentals, either out of your primary home or a separate investment property, you must make sure that your policy will allow for this. Only a handful of companies I'm aware of will offer this additional coverage. Call your insurance agent today, because there is a good chance any claim you make will be denied and your entire policy cancelled for nondisclosure of a material fact without this additional coverage. Just because you have a permit and show liability coverage to get your permit doesn't mean you're covered by your insurance company in the event of damage or lawsuit caused by an Airbnb guest.

Some insurance companies will provide policies endorsed for short-term rental, but you need to know what you're buying. Just like the preceding examples, many are written on ACV basis, but a select few can be written on Full or Extended Replacement Cost.

If you run an "owner-occupied short-term rental," in which you are using your home as a for-profit venture, that business is not covered by many homeowner's policies—period. If you think you might be "gaming the system," file a claim caused by a guest and see what happens.

I have quite a few clients who have Airbnb and VRBO guests who rent part of their primary residence. Once again you must have the right company that will offer the coverage needed to do this. One underwriter whose company will not offer this coverage told me that "if I find out that an insured is doing Airbnb in their home, I will issue a cancellation notice immediately." As with any insurance matter, let the buyer beware! Know what you're buying and get it in writing.

Insuring Vacant Dwellings

The last factor to consider regarding landlord insurance is what to do with vacant dwellings, most commonly held during a house-flipping project. This is the most expensive type of dwelling insurance out there—some companies offer these; some do not. Why is it so expensive to insure flips in progress? Vacancy risk plays a huge role because of the potential exposure to people roaming on the property while it's being renovated, vandalism, theft, and so on. Ever had an HVAC unit stolen? Yeah, I've paid that claim. Often, a variety of subcontractors (licensed or not) will be working on the home, and they can sue the owner if they get hurt on the job.

House flips can be major moneymakers, but you've got to protect yourself all the way through the process. I typically recommend insuring the property monthly for the finished value, including materials and labor, and it's been a good strategy so far. Just remember: it's best to have a personal comprehensive insurance agency take care of all aspects of this venture.

CHAPTER 6

FLOOD INSURANCE: DON'T LET YOUR MONEY FLOAT AWAY

*L*IKE IT OR NOT, WE ARE HAVING MORE AND MORE natural disasters in this country than ever before. Call it global warming, call it acts of God, call it whatever you want. If I had laid $1,000 on the table at the start of 2010 and wanted to bet anyone that Nashville, Tennessee, would experience a 1,000-year flood, everyone I know would have taken that "fool's bet."

And they'd have lost.

The *Tennessean* reported the two-day rainfall totals of May 1 and 2, 2010, exceeded thirteen inches.[2] I remember being at a Jimmy Buffett concert at Bridgestone Arena the night of Saturday, May 1, thinking, *Wow, the rain hasn't stopped all day*. The Cumberland River crested at 51.8 feet, well above its average of 30 to 33 feet.[3] Stormwater drains could not funnel the water fast enough. Neighborhoods saw kayakers going down their streets. Old Hickory Dam was within a foot of floodwaters cresting the dam, so the

Army Corps of Engineers had no choice but to release the water. This sent 420 billion gallons of water downstream,[4] which destroyed the Opryland Hotel and Opry Mills shopping mall before flowing directly into downtown Nashville. Look it up. It was awful.

People learned that the beautiful Harpeth River, which snakes in and around western Davidson County and into Williamson County, turned into an ugly, raging, uncontrolled flow of floodwater that took days to subside. Nearly 11,000 properties were either damaged or destroyed. We saw nearly $2 billion in private property damage and an estimated $247 million of public infrastructure damage.[5] Many people living in high-risk flood zones had either cancelled or not renewed their flood policies.

Two years later, in 2012, I had an office in one of Nashville's premier real estate firms, and Realtors were constantly asking me if a specific property was in a flood zone. They wanted to see if there had been any damage to a home for sale before showing it to their clients. I have access to the Federal Emergency Management Agency (FEMA) database of properties and can run zone determinations to see if flood insurance was required on a certain property. Also, I have access to Comprehensive Loss Underwriting Exchange (CLUE) reports, which is the property and casualty industry report of all of the claims associated with a specific person or address. They generally go back three or four years, so I could advise them on any flood-related claims on that property. It really helped their buyers make better, more informed decisions on their home purchases.

Who Issues Flood Insurance?

Flood insurance is controlled by the Federal Emergency Management Agency (FEMA). When you purchase a flood insurance policy, it is FEMA doing business as XYZ or ABC Insurance Company. They control the rates, the underwriting, and the premiums. An "AE" flood zone is the highest-rated zone. If you are financing a home with that rating with a mortgage company, they'll require flood insurance.

It's important to know that even if only *part* of the structure is in the flood zone, the entire structure is considered in the flood zone. Case in point: a condominium building in downtown Nashville is in close proximity to the Cumberland River. About 200 square feet of a 20,000-square-foot four-story building is in the flood zone. That means a condo on the top floor, as far away from the river as you can be, requires flood insurance because of that 200 square feet.

The premium cost of flood insurance depends completely on the elevation levels and how FEMA prices each particular risk. I have seen AE zone properties in the mid-$600/year range and also in the $4,000–$5,000/year range. It all depends.

As an experienced financial advisor, I would ask you how badly you want a home that has an AE zone rating. Is it enough to pay the mandatory flood insurance premium? Enough to recognize what might happen, in terms of emotional and financial distress caused by a flood? I can't answer those questions for you, but I can tell you what I'd think if it were me: *How much more home could I purchase if I used those premium dollars toward a different house without the need for flood insurance?*

Recently, Nashville had a weather event that caused a lot of water damage. We had a deluge of rain over a weekend. It was nothing like 2010, but it caused a lot of client concern. I was fielding calls from clients all Sunday morning saying, "There's a foot of water in my crawl space," or, "We have three creeks overflowing in our backyard and it's destroying our shed and outdoor bar!" It got so crazy I posted a two-minute video on social media to educate people that, without flood insurance, most of this damage was not covered.

A mantra I use to teach people the limits of the standard homeowner's insurance policy is *falling water is covered, rising water is not.* Meaning, falling rain, snow, hail, sleet, and ice are covered by the standard home insurance policy. Groundwater, pooling, or rising water is not.

Of the many calls I fielded that weekend, one comment in particular blew me away. A client told me that her former insurance agent informed her that she wasn't *allowed* to buy flood insurance because she wasn't in a flood zone. Totally incorrect! Anyone can buy flood insurance, and preferred risk policies are available to anyone not in a flood zone. The annual premium runs in the $400–$500 range.

Prevention versus Coverage

If you are a homeowner, here's something to consider. You've heard the saying, "An ounce of prevention is worth a pound of cure." A trip to the hardware store and a weekend of digging trenches can make all the difference for you in a weather event. I have French drains all around my home. You know, those five-inch black plastic drainpipes you attach to your downspouts? During that weekend of heavy rain, they pulled the water away from the front and sides of my home. Without those drains, though, my basement could have been filled with seeping groundwater and insurance would not have covered that. (By the way, basements aren't covered by flood policies anyway—only the main floors are.) If this has ever happened to you, it's worth the weekend installing the drainage system.

What about Your Car?

As I mentioned in chapter 2, damage caused by a flood is covered under the comprehensive portion of your auto policy. Here's why that matters: when a client called me recently to file a flood insurance claim (she was in a flood zone and had the appropriate policy), she also mentioned, "By the way, I can't find my car! It got swept away in the floodwaters."

You can't make this stuff up.

I told her when she finds it, it's covered under comprehensive. She sent me pictures later that day. She found the car. It was far down the street ... stuck in a tree.

CHAPTER 7

A QUICK WORD ON DEDUCTIBLES

*I*N THE INTRODUCTION TO THIS BOOK, I MADE A COMMENT about "recapturing and redeploying" the dollars that fly out the window every month. Throughout my career in the insurance industry, I've found that one of the greatest wastes of people's money is the mismanagement of the deductibles on their auto and property insurance coverage.

The lower the deductible, say for an auto collision, the less your out-of-pocket cost will be if you have a claim. However, the lower the deductible, the *higher* the annual premium will be. So, with a lower deductible, you end up paying more in premiums for the *chance* to pay less in deductibles *if* you have an accident. Let's break down what that might look like for a typical person.

Say you've carried $100 deductibles for comprehensive and collision on your autos for the last twenty years. The annual premium averages $1,000 per year. You've never filed a claim.

Had you carried $1,000 deductibles for the last twenty years, the annual premium would have been $600. That's

$400 per year you've given the insurance company for the *opportunity* to pay less *if* you file a claim.

Now, multiply that $400 by the twenty years you've been insured, and you see that you've paid $8,000 for the lower deductible even though you never needed it. That money is gone, never to return. But what if you had held on to that money? That $400 per year, if invested at only a 5 percent rate of return, would be worth nearly $14,000 after twenty years. So, you didn't just lose $8,000; you lost $14,000 or more!

$400/year × 20 years = $8,000 × 5% average annual return = $14,000+

This is called a *lost opportunity cost*, and it's something to consider across all your insurances. I'll talk a lot more about this in the Castles section on personal savings. You've heard financial entertainers talk about establishing an "emergency fund." Deductibles are a perfect example of what you would use that fund for!

If, through the course of this book, we can find multiple instances of money leaving your life unnecessarily, how much better off would you be? Remember this as we move forward into future chapters—especially when we get to the chapter on budgets!

CHAPTER 8

YOU BET YOUR LIFE (INSURANCE)

Have you ever seen a TV commercial boast, "A forty-year-old man can get $500,000 of high-quality life insurance of a ten-year term for only $15 per month"? They show him playing with his young kids. They assume he's in 100 percent perfect health and qualified for the best underwriting classification, but what does "high quality" even mean? And why would a forty-year-old father buy ten-year term in the first place? If he makes $250,000 a year in income, he would be leaving his family two times his annual salary. Really?

Red flags are flying big-time when I see these ads. The life insurance industry is playing the auto insurance game: selling strictly on price. It drives me insane.

Life insurance is one of the most criticized, scrutinized, misunderstood financial products ever invented. This is an industry in which no two people—even insurance professionals—can ever seem to agree on anything. Term life? Group term life through your employer? Whole life? Universal life? Too much? Not enough? Company ABC? Company XYZ? Pundits, consumers, salespeople, and financial entertainers all seem to have a strong opinion on the best way to insure your life. And so do I.

Google "life insurance," and you'll find more than a billion results! This chapter *could* make up 50 percent of this whole book—or we could keep it to one really good chapter. That matches the kinds of conversations I have with clients about this stuff every day. Some clients want to know the complex ins and outs, and others just want a simple, solid, high-level overview to help them make a good decision. For this book, though, I will err on the side of simplicity. My goal is to keep the potentially scary topic of life insurance as clear and unintimidating as possible. Here are the big questions to ask yourself when choosing life insurance.

How Much Do You Need?

There's the right way and the wrong way to determine how much life insurance you need. The right way is how the life insurance industry calculates that amount, a concept called *Human Life Value*. Remember how *Replacement Value* works in property insurance? Same concept.

The insurance industry uses this formula to determine how much life insurance a person can qualify for and should purchase.

- **Age 25–40:** 30 times annual income
- **Age 40–50:** 20 times annual income
- **Age 50–60:** 10 times annual income
- **Age 60+:**   1 times net worth

Do some quick math and I bet you'll find you are grossly underinsured using this industry method. You're probably thinking that's a big number. Yes, if you're in your twenties, thirties, or forties, it might be. But think of it this way: If your house burns to the ground, you've got enough coverage to rebuild it. If you die due to accident or sickness, shouldn't you have enough coverage to rebuild your family's life after you're gone?

The court system uses the same *Human Life Value* method, but they also build in the future values of what you would have earned had you lived. Remember that wreck I was involved in? Let's say I'd died in the accident and my family took that girl to court. I was still in my forties at the time, and we'll say my annual income was $100,000.

Using the preceding formula for someone in their forties, the court would have estimated my *Human Life Value* at twenty times my annual income: 20 × $100,000 = $2 million. They also would have added an estimated 4 to 5 percent rate of return on that amount, bringing the court judgment of my "value" up to $2.5 million, which is higher than the insurance industry uses. If you were in that situation, wouldn't you want your family to be awarded that much in the event of your death?

The wrong way to determine how much life insurance you need is the SWAG method. This is what most people use in their financial planning. SWAG stands for *Scientific Wild @$$ Guess*, meaning you pulled a nice round number out of the sky and that's the economic decision you made for your family. Can you smell the sarcasm? Insuring your life isn't a guessing game. You don't want to leave your family scrambling to make ends meet with a life insurance benefit based on what you thought sounded good.

The Four Phases of Your Financial Life

So, if I agree that term life is a great product and often the best answer for insuring one's life and protecting their loved ones, why even bother with other permanent life options, like whole life and cash value? I can explain by walking you through a typical financial planning scenario. Years ago, I was noodling around on a whiteboard and came up with this graph. (I love whiteboards, by the way.) I've found myself drawing it for almost every client when showing their life from a financial and insurance perspective. It's part of the job when you're a professional explainer like me.

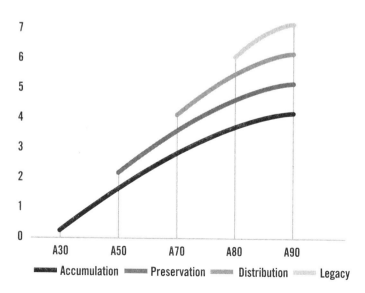

This chart shows the progression of the four phases of your financial life:

1. Accumulation
2. Preservation
3. Distribution
4. Legacy

Let's walk through these phases, and I'll explain what I mean by each.

Accumulation stage. At the start of your adult life, throughout your twenties, thirties, and forties, you will be almost exclusively in the *accumulation* stage. As you see on the graph, you'll never graduate from this phase; you'll be accumulating for the rest of your life by growing assets in savings accounts, retirement accounts, and other investments. Your risk tolerance will change as you age, and you likely won't have the same aggressive investment nature you had when you started out, but you should continue to fully invest in these accounts (based on time frame and risk tolerance) so the rate of return will keep up with inflation, taxes, and so on. When you take your last breath, your assets will be doing all they can to still gain a reasonable rate of return, whatever that is.

Preservation stage. Around age fifty, and after a few market corrections, the aggressive-growth investment style you've possibly had throughout your working lifetime starts to get a little more conservative, maybe shifting to a moderate-growth allocation. The focus at this stage is *preservation*. Even though you're still accumulating, you think it's a good idea to get just a little more conservative to protect the wealth you've built as you get closer to retirement, when you'll depend on it for your income. If you remember the market volatility of 2008, you know what I'm talking about!

Distribution stage. At age seventy, the IRS comes into play and says, "You've deferred these retirement accounts [IRA, 401(k), profit sharing] for a long time, and now it's time for you to start drawing out of those accounts. This is the start of the *distribution* phase, when the government requires you to start taking your *required minimum distribution*. Even though you're now semi-, quasi-, or fully retired, your assets are still rolling along in the accumulation and preservation stages. You don't leave those phases; you just keep entering new phases.

Legacy phase. Now, you're retired. You have accumulated some assets. If you're like many retirees, you never feel like you have *enough*, but it is where you are at the time. Social Security benefits have kicked in for you and your spouse, your home is hopefully paid for or has a very small mortgage balance, and you're ready to enjoy your golden years. Are you at the end of the financial phases? No!

Hopefully, you have a heart and a soul, along with a wonderful family of children, grandchildren, and maybe even great-grandchildren. So now, you're thinking about the *legacy* phase. No, I'm not talking about putting your name on a building; I'm just talking about leaving this world a little better than you found it. Call it a "legacy of love," as that's what my dad left me and my family. This is, most likely, the phase where your life insurance decisions will make the greatest impact on those you leave behind.

What You Need to Know about Term Life Insurance

Traditional planners and financial entertainers have the same recommendation almost 100 percent of the time: "Buy term life insurance and invest what you would otherwise be 'overpaying' on cash value insurance. Never buy any type of permanent cash value building life insurance. It's a horrible investment, and the only reason the agent recommends it is because of the high commissions." However, my perspective is a little different.

Depending on where you are in your life cycle, the type of insurance you should buy is usually pretty simple. If you are in your twenties to early fifties and near your highest income potential, term insurance will be the most affordable option. Yes, I do recommend it more often than not. The longest term policy available during those years is the thirty-year guaranteed level, meaning the premium is guaranteed not to change for thirty years. This type of policy will get you as close to your *Human Life Value* as possible. If you're over fifty, there are other strategies to consider that I'll explain later.

There are a few optional benefits that I always build into term life insurance policies. If you are shopping on www.SuperCheapTermLife.com (not a real site…yet), they will never mention these options because they might cost a few extra dollars per month, but they are absolutely worth adding to your policy.

Waiver of Premium: If you become disabled and have this rider on your life insurance policy, depending on the definitions of disability in the policy, the premiums can be waived and the insurance company will make the payments on your behalf for the length of your disability or the length of the policy term. Think of it this way: If you are sick or hurt and cannot work, what is one of the first expenses you're going to eliminate? Yes, the life insurance premium is almost the first thing to go, but you'll be giving up your protection altogether. With this waiver, problem solved.

Extended Conversion Rider: Depending on which company you choose, this benefit is a part of the actual policy and is spelled out in the policy language. Some term insurance policies do not offer this, so it's important to confirm this with prospective providers when you're deciding which policy to purchase.

At any point in the policy's term, any or all of the face amount can be converted to a permanent cash value building policy with no medical evidence required. This is a key part of the term policy I always show the client for this reason: I've worked with one awesome couple for almost thirty years. More than twenty years ago, I wrote $250,000 term policies on each one of them. It was what fit their financial plan. Then, she was diagnosed with cancer—one month before her term life insurance expired. Because of this rider, we were able to convert the expiring term policy to a universal life policy that would remain in force for the duration of her life for the full $250,000 benefit. In fact, because no medical evidence was required, she was even given *preferred nonsmoker* status, which is how the term policy had been originally issued two decades earlier.

Was it a little more expensive? Yes. Could she have bought another term policy? Absolutely not. The cancer diagnosis had made her totally uninsurable at that point. Sadly, she died two years later … and we all hurt together. This was one of the first death benefit checks I personally delivered: $250,000 to the husband, 100 percent tax-free. It still hurts as I write this.

Accelerated Death Benefit Rider: This rider came into play during and after the AIDS crisis in the '80s. Many men who had no health insurance but had life insurance were selling their death benefits for cash settlements to pay for their medical care. This rider says that if you are deemed to have a terminal illness by a qualified medical professional, a percentage of the death benefits can be paid to you as a living benefit to take care of medical expenses, family needs or wishes, or to have a higher quality of living while you're still here to enjoy it.

How Term Life Can Work Together with Riders

Now, let's look at how these three term life options can work in concert. We'll say at thirty-five years old, making $100,000 per year, I purchase a guaranteed level twenty-year term life insurance policy with all three of these riders. The face amount is my *Human Life Value* of $3 million (30 times my annual income of $100,000).

Ten years later, I am involved in a terrible car accident and am declared permanently disabled at age forty-five. *Waiver of Premium* keeps the term policy in force at no cost to me. The insurance company starts paying my premiums for me and continues to do so throughout the term. My life expectancy is unknown at the time, but my quality of life is severely diminished.

At age fifty-five, my level term premium will expire, but I execute the *Extended Conversion Rider* and keep all or a part of the $3 million face amount I choose by converting the term to a "nonterm" policy (for example: universal life, whole life, and so on). I get to keep the preferred best rating I originally qualified for with zero medical evidence needed.

At age sixty, I am told I have less than eighteen months to live by a qualified physician. My policy has an *Accelerated Death Benefit Rider*, which allows me and my family to access a portion of the $3 million death benefit while I'm living. As such, the *death* benefit can be used as a *living* benefit while I'm still here, and it remains 100 percent tax-free.

So, a properly structured term insurance policy will pay for itself if I get disabled; if I'm deemed terminal, the death benefit can be accessed while I'm living; and if it looks like I'll barely outlive the term, I can convert it to a permanent cash value policy to make sure my family still gets the benefit. That's a solid life insurance plan. Is that the kind of coverage you have? Probably not, if price is the only thing you look at when you buy insurance. And not if you get all your insurance advice from advisors who don't specialize in the nuances of life insurance and the available riders.

It's important to mention that any group term life insurance policy you have should only be considered icing on the cake and should never be considered your main life insurance policy. What happens if you become sick and cannot qualify for a personally owned policy . . . and then you lose your job? Think about it for a moment. You'll be completely stuck. It's important to buy well-structured, personal life insurance from financially strong companies while you're still healthy and active. It's amazing to me when someone qualifies with the best health ratings, but they do not buy insurance. Conversely, when someone is completely uninsurable for a new personally owned policy, they will pay whatever it takes to get whatever coverage they can get!

When Permanent Life Insurance Makes Sense

However, you may have painted yourself into a corner without knowing it. Remember the legacy phase I described earlier? By using the strategies of the financial entertainers who say, "Only buy term life insurance and invest the difference," you might find yourself thinking:

- I've spent my lifetime accumulating assets for retirement and have outlived my term life insurance policies. There is no more life insurance for my spouse, so how do I have that conversation?
- I've stayed the course through market corrections, financial downturns, market crashes, and no telling how many career and job changes.
- I've put two kids through school and gotten them both married off.
- What happens if we get sick and need in-home or nursing care?
- Have I planned for the possibility of outliving our nest egg?
- Do I have a plan to make sure my spouse is taken care of when I die?

Welcome to the world of traditional financial planning! This is what much of the Internet is teaching you to do, as well as many financial planners. So, let's play this out using some of the strategies I teach my clients.

The traditional "buy term and invest the difference" advice *does* make sense . . . for a while. Buying term insurance with a face amount of your *Human Life Value* and investing into tax-favored retirement plans is a great plan when you're younger, during the accumulation and preservation phases of your life. The problem is, it's not such a wise move as you age into the distribution and legacy stages.

So using my preceding example, let's say I'm actively investing into my retirement and brokerage accounts from the day I purchase my guaranteed level thirty-year term life insurance with *Waiver of Premium*, *Extended Conversion Rider*, and *Accelerated Death Benefit* included. As a healthy nonsmoker, I got the best insurance class available and the lowest annual premium, even with the additional riders.

From ages thirty-five to sixty-five, I am optimally insured to protect my family against my premature death, but (and this is a *big* but) let's say my strategy of asset growth is nowhere close to what my projections were when I started this plan. Life got in the way of my best-case-scenario planning. For example:

- I was laid off once and downsized once.
- I had to take care of and financially support my aging parents.
- I had to take a premature withdrawal from my IRAs to pay for an emergency.

- I got divorced (and maybe remarried).
- I suffered through the market correction in 2008, made an irrational decision, and pulled my money out of the market, completely missing the double-digit run-up that came afterward.
- My plan assumed an average annual return of 8 to 10 percent, but it's actually averaged a little more than 4 percent over the long haul.
- I've had a health scare or two, and I can no longer get the ultra-preferred rating I once had.

All this to say, that targeted seven-figure account balance your financial calculator gave you is coming up a bit short. You're worried about not having enough money for your spouse and yourself in retirement, not to mention what happens if you get sick or die younger than expected.

What happened to that grandiose plan of living a comfortable retirement, having enough money to do what you want to do when you want to do it, not outliving your money, and leaving a legacy of love to your heirs?

But what if, the year before your thirty-year level term life insurance policy expired, knowing that you were entering the distribution and legacy phases of your life, you exercised the *Extended Conversion Rider* of your term policy for a reasonable portion of that policy that you could keep for the rest of your life? Let's say that you and your advisor agreed that it was financially feasible to "convert" $250,000 of the $1 million term policy.

At that point, you're not concerned with *Human Life Value* anymore; you're concerned with your life in retirement.

When you die, regardless of what is left in your distribution bucket, it gets replenished 100 percent tax-free with the life insurance proceeds.

All those term premiums you paid over all those years will be recaptured, and your family will remember the legacy of love you leave behind. This is a simple strategy, and it all starts with purchasing the right type of term insurance with the right optional riders from the right life insurance professional. This is one of my biggest biases, by the way—and the reason I disagree with what the financial entertainers and a large majority of financial planners say about permanent life insurance.

All Permanent Life Products Are Not the Same

A misconception I often hear repeated is that anything that isn't *term life insurance* is *whole life insurance*. That is entirely untrue. *Whole life* is just one of many permanent options, but it's the one everyone seems to rail against. Financial entertainers typically detest whole life insurance or anything remotely resembling it, such as universal life or variable universal life, primarily because they don't understand it.

Despite what you hear from those entertainers, there are many types of permanent life insurance and many reasons for choosing them. They are more expensive than term, so they can be seen as luxury products. For my clients whose monthly cash flow prohibits whole life insurance or who need a larger death benefit, I recommend term insurance. But that certainly doesn't mean permanent insurance has no place in a well-structured financial plan.

Isn't it funny how whole life policies worked amazingly well for all Americans up until the early '80s when these things called "mutual funds" came along with the opportunity for higher returns? That's when the advice to "buy term and invest the difference" became popular.

The other two types of permanent life insurance I see regularly are *Universal Life* and *Variable Universal Life* policies. In a nutshell, *Universal Life* is buying a death benefit and investing the difference in a side fund that has a fixed interest rate adjusted annually by the company. This is the most prevalent permanent life policy being sold today.

Variable Universal Life is the same concept, except the difference is invested into a grouping of subaccounts of your choosing. These are great when we're in a bull market. However, when it slows and your cash values diminish with the stock market, you've got to remember: it's still life insurance and the premiums have to be paid.

An attractive feature with these types of policies that you should consider is that you have two death benefit options. Option One will pay the death benefit *only*, and the cash values technically become a part of that death benefit. This has its place if I'm focused on death benefit only at the most affordable premium. Option Two will pay the death benefit *plus* the cash value. This strategy can be more expensive from a premium perspective, but it's attractive to the beneficiaries because they receive the death benefit 100 percent tax-free *and* receive the cash values (including appreciation) 100 percent tax-free.

The Good, the Bad, and the Ugly

I've probably sold every type of life insurance product at some point in my almost forty-year career, including whole life, universal life, variable universal life, and term insurance. I know the good, the bad, and the ugly about each product. There are great products to choose from, and there are bad— just like there are really great advisors out there, along with some really bad ones! What's the old adage? "If all you have to sell is a hammer, everyone looks like a nail!"

We've covered a lot of ground in this chapter, so let me wrap up with a few final thoughts and reminders:

- Life insurance is the only financial product I know of that could be considered both a moat *and* a castle. Its primary purpose is protection, but there are plenty of options to help you build and grow your castle along the way.
- Term life is a great option when you're younger and if you only need it for a specific time frame. However, you shouldn't *only* look at term when putting your total plan together. There are other options that could make a big difference.
- When choosing your life insurance policy, look for the three options I mentioned: Waiver of Premium, Extended Conversion Rider, and Accelerated Death Benefit. Even if you want to stick to a term-only strategy for most of your life, these riders, if explained properly, could benefit you greatly either if a life event happens or if your current financial plan doesn't work out the way you hope.

- Remember that everyone has a bias. Life insurance agents have a bias toward cash value-building policies, and financial advisors have a bias toward term insurance. Know the difference between the two and why you'd personally choose one over the over.
- Think past the advertising. Just because you recognize a company's name and mascot doesn't mean it's the right choice for you.
- There's a time and a place for both types of policies.

I don't blame people for getting confused about all the options out there, especially when you hear such…*powerful*…opinions coming from the financial entertainers. I get it. Life insurance is complicated, and that's why you shouldn't just make a blanket decision about one type of coverage versus another. You need to work with a professional who takes all the variables of your life into consideration in coming up with a personalized plan. After all, you don't need a life insurance plan that works for *everybody*; you need one that works specifically for you and your family.

Oh, regarding the commission argument. Herein lies a big part of the problem with all the pitfalls I've discussed throughout the Moats section. That is, every insurance product I've covered so far, with the exception of disability income, renews either every six months or annually, so you're forced to at least look at the coverages you've chosen and the policies you own. You're always "shopping" for new coverage (aka, trying to save money) and looking for the best deal. All these types of policies have premiums guaranteed only one year at a time, and they are always changing as the insurance companies continue their endless onslaught of advertising.

Life insurance, however, usually does not renew every year. You buy a guaranteed level premium for ten, fifteen, twenty, or thirty years. Any commissions paid are usually fully paid in the first year and a very low percentage on renewal, if any at all. Rarely will the person who sold you that policy two decades earlier ever reach out to you. So, the premiums go on automatic payments, the actual policy is nowhere to be found, and then one day, you find it again. Only to realize what you thought you bought is not what you actually own.

Analyze Your Coverage

Now, it's time for me to potentially stress you out a little bit. Let's take a quick look at how much life insurance you currently have (if any) versus what you now know you need. Fill in the blanks below.

- I am currently age _____
- My annual income is $_____
- My *Human Life Value,* based on the chart a few pages ago, is $_____
- I currently own $_____ in life insurance
- Based on my answers I am underinsured by $_____

How does it look? How do you feel right now? Is it time to call your agent and upgrade your policy?

Quick Review

Using the **Human Life Value** method, what is the maximum
amount of life insurance I can qualify for? _____

How much do I own now? _____

_____

Do I have a **Waiver of Premium** benefit on my life policy? _____

_____

Do I have an **Extended Conversion Rider** on my life policy? ___

_____

Do I have an **Accelerated Death Benefit Rider** on my policy? _

_____

Scale of 1–10 on the confidence scale … how do I feel right now? ___

_____

QUESTIONS FOR THOUGHT

Do I remember why I bought the amount of coverage I own? _____

_____

Do I remember who sold it to me or what website I bought it from? __

_____

Are my beneficiaries correct and current? _____

_____

What is my plan for this policy as I get older? _____

_____

Who can I trust to review what I have without trying to sell me another
policy? _____

_____

_____

_____

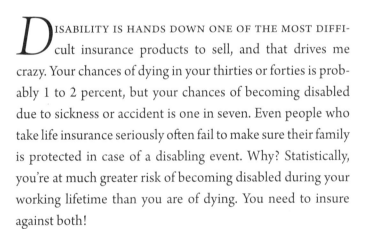

CHAPTER 9

EXPECT THE UNEXPECTED: DISABILITY INCOME PLANS

D ISABILITY IS HANDS DOWN ONE OF THE MOST DIFFI-
cult insurance products to sell, and that drives me
crazy. Your chances of dying in your thirties or forties is probably 1 to 2 percent, but your chances of becoming disabled
due to sickness or accident is one in seven. Even people who
take life insurance seriously often fail to make sure their family
is protected in case of a disabling event. Why? Statistically,
you're at much greater risk of becoming disabled during your
working lifetime than you are of dying. You need to insure
against both!

I've heard all the objections:
- "I have it at work, so I don't need it."
- "That will never happen to me!"
- "Hey, it's not like I'm a high-rise window-washer! I'll
  be fine!"

Despite the protestations, I've learned there are really *two* prices for disability income policies: the price you pay if you buy…and the price you pay if you don't.

Most disability plans, either individually owned or company-provided, will pay a benefit equal to 60 percent of your income. Why? Because that's a good estimate of what your current gross income would be minus taxes, Social Security, and all the other little hits your typical paycheck takes before it lands in your bank account. But is 60 percent really enough? And how long will that benefit last? There are so many questions in the world of disability, and too few people actually *ask* those questions.

One of the challenges in selling disability income plans is the inherent fuzziness of the very definition of the term *disability*. You don't see this in any other types of insurance. Life insurance is simple: there's a death certificate. Auto insurance is simple: the police report shows who is at fault. But disability insurance? Who determines what *disabled* means in your situation? That's where it gets tricky.

When buying personal disability income plans, you're basically buying a book of definitions. There are a multitude of definitions for the many different types of disability you might experience, from physical to mental. There are two key occupational categories to consider: your *own* occupation and *any* occupation.

These are crucial to understand. Here's a good example: Two people, Bert and Ernie, work for the same company. Let's say they are both forty-year-old commercial bankers.

Both make a base salary of $75,000 ($6,250/month) plus an annual bonus of $150,000 ($12,500/month), making their total monthly income $18,750/month.

So, same age, same job, same income.

Now, one day Bert and Ernie walk to lunch together and, while crossing a busy downtown street, both are hit and critically injured by a truck that ran a red light. Both are considered "permanently disabled" and will not be going to work for a long while, if ever again.

Bert only has the group disability plan provided by his employer, which is 60 percent of his base salary. Ernie, however, called his agent when he got the job at the bank because he realized that the group benefits provided at work covered his base salary only (not his actual income, including bonuses), and he bought a supplemental individual disability policy.

Here's how it plays out:

- **BERT:** After six months (a typical waiting period in disability cases), Bert qualifies for disability benefits of 60 percent of his base salary only.
  - $75,000 × 60% = $45,000 / 12 months = $3,750/month
  - In addition, since the bank deducted the disability plan costs as an employee benefit expense, the benefit to Bert is *taxable* as ordinary income. So, he'll net around $3,000/month.
  - **RESULT:** Bert goes from making $18,500/month to roughly $3,000/month. But wait; it'll get worse in a minute.

- **ERNIE:** After six months, Ernie also qualifies for disability benefits.
  - As a bank employee, Ernie gets the same benefit as Bert of approximately $3,000/month.
  - But his individual disability plan will now also be enacted due to his total disability, which will pay him an additional $10,000/month. Since Ernie does not deduct the personal insurance premium, his benefits are 100 percent tax-free.
  - **RESULT:** Ernie gets the same $3,000/month from his work disability plan *plus* $10,000/month (tax-free) from his additional disability plan until age sixty-five. Combined, this gives him a monthly income of $13,750.

Both guys take a pay cut, but Ernie can probably get by on $13,750/month. Bert, however, is now making one-sixth of what he used to make. You think that's going to cut it, especially with the extra hardship of his new disability?

If that weren't bad enough for ol' Bert, remember when I said his situation was going to get worse? Well, I said that there are two occupational categories for disability: *your occupation* and *any occupation*. Here's what that means. A disability policy for *any occupation* means that if Bert and Ernie can perform *any* job—even pushing a broom or bagging groceries—then they are no longer considered disabled. That's the kind of policy the bank provided its employees. So, after twenty-four months, if Bert and Ernie can perform any occupation, they lose their disability income. At the two-year mark, then, they both lose the $3,000/month from the bank policy, leaving Bert with zero income. He will have to find some kind of job he can perform to make ends meet.

Ernie, however, isn't facing such a nightmare. The policy his agent sold him was defined as a *"your occupation"* plan. That means he will receive disability payments if he's deemed unable to perform his specific former duties as a commercial banker. So even though Ernie loses the $3,000/month benefit from the bank plan, he still gets to receive the $10,000/month tax-free benefit from his additional disability plan until retirement age.

Which one of these guys would you rather be?

The Five Bases You Should Be Sure to Cover

Whenever I talk to someone about disability coverage, I always try to cover these five bases. First, if you are working for a company that provides group disability benefits, have someone review the definitions. *Any occupation* is standard language in these contracts, usually after a twenty-four-month period. You may *think* you're covered long-term only to find yourself looking for a new career after two years.

Second, triple-check what sources of income your work policy covers. I've seen the preceding scenario multiple times where bonus and commissions were not covered. If you're in sales or any profession that includes some kind of variable income component, you need to be comparing your potential disability benefits to your *actual* working income. And, if you're self-employed, your benefit may be calculated on your taxable income, not your gross income.

Third, many insurance advisors try to sell the maximum benefit for the maximum period. I regularly see a ninety-day waiting period and 60 percent of total income to age sixty-seven. Many people never realize you can tweak each one of these factors to land on a policy that's just right for you. You can lengthen the waiting period, shorten the benefit period, and reduce the monthly dollar amount. Take some time, look at your basic expenses, and customize the plan to fit your budget. After all, a little bit of something is better than a whole lot of nothing!

Fourth, disability income plans are the hardest to qualify for. Case in point: You see a chiropractor regularly because you need adjustments due to your golf game and generally active lifestyle. You've also had a knee scoped. Finally, because of the stresses of daily life, your physician has prescribed a mild antidepressant. End result? Your disability policy is issued but has exclusions for your back, your knee, and any mental and nervous conditions, meaning you can't claim disability for any of those preexisting conditions.

Fifth, many providers offer an additional benefit for millennials that will cover student debt. It's generally waived at death, but not in the event of disability by sickness or accident. A disabling event could therefore leave you unable to work but still buried under a pile of unpaid student loans. So, consider purchasing a plan to cover your student debt payments—especially if you have graduate or postgraduate debt with higher interest rates.

Disabling accidents and illnesses are a tragic yet common part of life. You may not be able to avoid becoming disabled, but you *can* decide whether it wrecks your financial life. You just have to make that choice *before* it happens!

CHAPTER 10

SHOULD YOU CARE ABOUT LONG-TERM CARE?

Nuews flash: you're getting older. So are your parents...if they're still with us. With advancements in health care, Americans are living longer than ever these days, which is great! But it also presents a financial challenge for those who are unprepared for the rising costs of long-term and/or residential elder care. I would venture that someway, somehow, the conversation of care for either a parent, grandparent, your siblings, or yourself and your spouse has come to light. Industry statistics reveal that 70 percent of all Americans will require some form of care in their lifetimes. That means there's a solid chance you'll need it too. And *someone's* got to pay for it.

Modern medicine and scientific advances are giving us longer and longer life expectancies. In the early 1960s, my grandfather had several heart attacks that finally took him in his early seventies. Today, he would have had surgeries that could have extended his life another fifteen or twenty years. Thus, he probably would have needed some kind of ongoing care in his later years.

The insurance industry has a long history with all the types of insurance I've mentioned so far in this book. They use actuarial data to predict the possibilities of paying claims to their insureds, and that data is proven by the millions of people they've tracked over the years.

Where the insurance industry has decades, if not centuries, of data used by actuaries to price every product in the Moats section, they really have not figured out how to effectively price the cost of aging and the care needed as we age. Long-term care insurance plans have only been in existence since the late 1970s and really didn't catch on until the late 1980s and early 1990s, and only a handful of insurers offered the product then.

These policies became popular when the baby boomer generation started looking toward retirement. Because there was no data to use to price the products, policies were sold with very cost-effective premiums. A *lot* of people purchased these plans, many through their employer via payroll deduction.

However, as the baby boomers started needing care, the insurance companies quickly realized they weren't charging enough in premiums to meet their financial responsibilities and keep enough in reserves for anticipated claims and expenses. This caused a rush to correct—or *overcorrect*—their mistake. First, annual premiums increased exponentially as they were only guaranteed one year at a time. Second, policy benefits were reduced to adjust for those premium increases.

Third, many insurance companies stopped selling new policies altogether.

Assessing Your Need

Long-term care policies are expensive, and they're not something you can be sure you'll ever need. That makes these policies a prime target for early policy owner cancellation if the aging person's monthly budget starts getting tight. I totally understand that. In fact, I had this argument with my dad at least once a year for several years before he died.

In those times, I talked to Dad as a son, not as an agent. In fact, I have never managed my parents' financial affairs. I wanted them to be my *parents*, not my *clients*. However, I do have a close relationship with the man who does manage everything, and he and I talked about this issue often. He remains a dear friend to this day, and probably will be for the remainder of my days.

In the end, Dad died at age ninety-one without ever needing to go into a facility or have someone come to the house to oversee his care. His "life battery" just ran out. All those premiums he paid over the years went by the wayside. Mom still has the policy, and I now have the annual conversation with her. And the truth is, she has a good point. You may pay a small fortune in premiums for long-term care, and a lot of money that could be put toward your retirement income! Is this really the best we can do?

The modern solution lies within many of the permanent life insurance products being sold today, whether it's whole life, universal life, or variable life. Since these plans are with them for the rest of their lives, the insurance companies have made provisions for long-term care benefits *within* many permanent life insurance plans by creating additional policy riders that allow for these benefits. If a policyholder faces a long-term care situation, they are able to pay for their care by utilizing the provisions built into the death benefit defined in their life insurance policy.

To enact those living benefits of your life insurance policy, you'd need to qualify according to several factors. As a general rule, there are six Activities of Daily Living, also known as ADLs. If a doctor certifies that you are unable to perform two of the six ADLs, under the policy definitions, you qualify to receive care from your long-term care policy. The ADLs are:

1. Eating: Can you feed yourself?
2. Bathing and Hygiene: Can you bathe yourself and brush your teeth?
3. Dressing: Are you physically able to dress yourself?
4. Grooming: Can you keep your own nails trimmed, hair combed, and so on?
5. Mobility: Can you move without the need of a cane, walker, or wheelchair?
6. Continence: Are you able to go to the bathroom by yourself?

For example, consider my mom and dad. The great news about my dad's family is that we traditionally live long lives. My granddad Carden lived to age ninety—and he smoked three packs of Pall Mall unfiltered cigarettes for decades! The bad news is that our chances for needing long-term care are significant.

For many years, my dad and mom spent much of their money on long-term care policies. Over time, the premiums started getting out of control; then the company they were with stopped selling new policies altogether. Eventually their policies were sold to another company but remained in force as they could not be cancelled. As they aged, this process became increasingly more stressful.

When I once asked Dad what his greatest fear was, he said it was not having enough in savings and investments for Mom to be comfortable after he passed away. I agreed, and I advised him that if he cancelled his long-term care policy and then needed some form of permanent care, the cost could bankrupt him and Mom.

If my dad had the long-term care benefit in his life insurance policy, a portion of the death benefit would have become a *living benefit* they could have used for his care. Then, when he died, the unused portion of the death benefit would be paid to Mom 100 percent tax-free.[6]

For this reason, I strongly encourage anyone within ten years of retirement to own some form of permanent insurance in their moat. If structured properly, every premium dollar put into the policy will be used by either the policyholder or beneficiaries—whether as "tax-free living benefits" for long-term care, a loan or withdrawal of the accumulated cash values, or as death benefits that are 100 percent tax-free. To me, it's a good use of capital and a smart decision for the policyholder and their family. Did I mention that all of the benefits of a permanent life insurance policy can be used 100 percent tax-free?

CHAPTER 11

HEALTH INSURANCE: ENOUGH INSTABILTY TO MAKE YOU SICK

*A*LOT HAS CHANGED IN THE HEALTH CARE INDUSTRY over the last two presidencies, from the formation of the Affordable Care Act to the removal of the penalty for not having health care coverage. Current regulations state that individuals do not have to carry health insurance; however, going without any kind of health care is simply too great a risk for anyone to take on. Everyone needs at least some type of catastrophic coverage. Regardless of the premium, deductible, or benefits, you simply *must* have some type of plan in place to prevent financial disaster in the event of a significant health event, either through accident or illness.

As of 2019, a full two-thirds of all bankruptcies (66.5 percent) filed in the US were caused by medical debts that consumers cannot repay.[7]

Big castle, big moat, remember? Moats protect your assets and income. If you try to squeak by without health insurance, you're basically leaving the drawbridge down, leaving your castle open to attack.

CHAPTER 12

WILLS, WILLS, WILLS

D ISCLOSURE: I AM NOT AN ATTORNEY, NOR AM I
licensed to offer legal advice. But I have been in the
insurance and financial game for a long time, and I can give
you some common-sense advice. You ready? Here it is: *You
need a will. Now.*[8]

Legally speaking, dying without a will is called *intestacy.*
Practically speaking, dying without a will is called *irrespon-
sible.* If you die without a will in many states, such as my home
state of Tennessee, you assume your assets will automatically go to your closest relatives. The operative word in that
sentence is *assume* ... and we know what that spells. You had
your entire adult life to decide who gets what, and you didn't
do it. An important fact is that everyone has a will. You either
write it for yourself and your loved ones, or the government
writes it for you!

While a will is a critical piece of your financial puzzle, it's
not all you need for your and your loved ones' peace of mind.
Along with a will, you need other key legal documents in force

immediately, while you're still of sound mind. Specifically, you need to work with an attorney to establish a *durable power of attorney for health care and financial decisions.* This document names the person or persons to whom you grant full legal power to make decisions on your behalf regarding your health, lifesaving measures, and financial issues. This person might literally hold the power of life and death over you, so choose carefully!

Create a Will to Cover Your Assets

For example, let's say you're a young, single professional and you're sitting there thinking, *I don't have much money, and I have no dependents. Why do I need a will?*

I'm so glad you asked!

Picture this: You're healthy one minute and an hour later, you're in the emergency room in critical condition due to accident or illness. Let's say you were in a horrible car accident and have just been delivered by helicopter to the ER. You're unconscious, lying on a hospital bed, unable to make any decisions whatsoever. Now, what do you do? Well…nothing. You can't do anything; you're in a coma.

So, what does the emergency room doctor do? Where's he getting his instructions or directives? Who does he call? Does he keep you alive artificially in a coma for the next ten years, or does he let you pass away? If you die, are you going to be buried or cremated? Who is going to take care of your beloved puppy? Who gets your prized collection of Beatles vinyl? These are terrible questions to think about, but *someone* has to think about them.

The best person for the job is *you*. Only you can't make these decisions at this point. If you didn't put these choices in writing before your car accident, you lost your chance to call the shots. Are you starting to see the need for a will?

If you're married, everything I just said applies, but kick it up a few notches. If you're incapacitated, have you given someone express permission to make decisions on your behalf? Say you're a newly married couple. The house is in your name only, but you and your spouse are paying the mortgage together. What happens if you die? Does your spouse have proper legal ownership of the house? If you said, "Of course," you would be …*guessing.* The truth is, we can't answer that one way or the other right now. He or she might get the house. He or she might get kicked to the curb. Guess who gets to decide? The courts! Welcome to the endless limbo of probate.

Probate is the court process by which a will is proved valid or invalid. It's also where you have to go if there are no designations for successorship of specific assets. If you have a will, they just need to make sure everything is in order before they execute your final wishes. If you die without a will, things get . . . messier. Many of your assets will automatically be thrown into probate. Assets that are duly titled, such as homes or cars in both names, will normally flow smoothly through probate, as will investment accounts titled either "joint tenants with rights of survivorship" (JTWROS) or "transferable on death" (TOD).

Assets that have a beneficiary designation, such as retirement accounts [IRA, 401(k), profit sharing] and life insurance plans, or assets that are duly titled, should go directly to the named beneficiaries. In these cases, there is no need for probate. However, if you have specific assets such as individual stock portfolios, classic car collections, investment real estate, gold coins, or perhaps your primary residence . . . and the list goes on and on . . . those items have to go through probate.

I had lunch with Matthew, my estate planning attorney, one day. I asked him what he charged for a will and possibly a trust, and he explained that his fees are a one-time expense for the drafting and execution of these documents. Then I asked him about probate. He said his billable hour was between $250–$300, depending on the client, and that includes the time he spends just sitting and waiting in the courtroom to be heard. He said the average probate cost in his firm ranges from $3,500–$8,000, depending on the complexity and the time needed to completely probate the will.

If you have a blended family that includes a mix of natural kids and stepchildren, you can save them all from probate by making your wishes known now, while you still can. Probate court can be a special kind of hell when spouses, ex-spouses, children, and stepchildren are all vying for their piece of your pie. Some of the most complicated planning I've been a part of involves a couple who just got married for the third time each! They could have two totally separate sets of kids and grandkids. See the potential dilemma?

Covering Minor Children

Your will tells the court who you have named to be the guardian of your minor children. If you have a special needs child, this is even more urgent. In this situation, you aren't just talking about your health and possessions; you're talking about the long-term—possibly lifetime—care of your child. Who will take care of them? Where will they go? Who do you trust with the extra-large life insurance policy you've put in place to ensure their ongoing care when you're gone? How can you be sure they will get the best treatment and most loving home? There's only one way to be sure: by making those decisions yourself and having those conversations with your loved ones now. Do not spin the wheel on who will parent your child for the rest of his or her life. Make the call yourself—while you still can. This is where a competent attorney with expertise in wills and the creation of trusts earns every dime!

Consider a real-life experience that happened to me twice (personally *and* professionally): what happens if both spouses die simultaneously? When I was five, my Uncle George, Aunt Grace, and three cousins flew to Knoxville in a private plane to celebrate Thanksgiving with us. They didn't make it. The plane crashed, killing everyone aboard.

Years later, one of my favorite clients and his wife died in an auto accident one Sunday coming home from church. His wife was named as his beneficiary, but he did not have contingent beneficiaries named, which left the court to decide who their assets went to. It was awful, to say the least. I miss him.

Another scenario I'm seeing more often these days is the case of same-sex couples—married or not—who live together and own property and assets together. These rules are ever-changing and are different state to state, so do not trust the government to do what you'd *want* them to do. Again, make the arrangements yourself by putting your wishes in writing in the form of a will. And, of course, get your partner to do the same!

We've all heard the horror stories of celebrities dying without wills and the nightmares that followed: Elvis, Conway Twitty, and more recently, Prince. These get all kinds of attention because of the amount of wealth involved, but your own "wealth" is just as important, regardless of how much or how little you think you have. You have the power to save your loved ones from this madness. All it takes is a simple appointment with an attorney to get your (and your spouse's) will, living will, and power of attorney documents in order.

Essential point: *Put a will in place ASAP!* There are various websites that can handle the basics for you pretty cheaply (better than nothing), but you'll get the best, most personalized and complete service from a local attorney who specializes in wills, trusts, and estates. It'll cost you several hundred dollars, but like insurance, it's money you're spending to protect yourself, your loved ones, and your assets. Don't skip it.

Personal areas of review, thoughts, and reflections

Auto Insurance

_____

_____

_____

Home/Condo/Renters/Landlord Insurance

_____

_____

_____

Umbrella/Liability Insurance

_____

_____

_____

Life Insurance

_____

_____

_____

Disability Insurance

_____

_____

_____

Health Insurance

_____

_____

_____

Long-Term Care

_____

_____

_____

Wills, Powers of Attorney, Trusts _____
_____
_____
_____

People I need to talk with about what I've read and learned:

_____Spouse or Significant Other

_____Children

_____ Parents & Grandparents (if still alive)

_____ Brothers & Sisters

_____ Best Friends & Confidants

Action Items
_____
_____
_____
_____
_____

Additional Thoughts
_____
_____
_____
_____
_____
_____
_____
_____
_____

PART 2

CREATING YOUR CASTLE OF WEALTH

The best time to plant a tree was twenty years ago. The second-best time is now.

—CHINESE PROVERB

CHAPTER 13

YOUR CASTLE BLUEPRINT

WITH THE MOAT DISCUSSION OUT OF THE WAY, YOU may be thinking, *Oh boy, now we're getting to the fun stuff! I wonder what stock tips Brian is going to give me?* WRONG!

Because everyone thinks building wealth is so fun, they usually move way too fast, skipping the crucial first steps and failing to do the basic stuff first. But not you. Not anymore. If you've gotten to this point in the book, now you know that you have to dig your moat before you do *any* construction on your castle. Or, to put it more directly, you shouldn't do *anything* in this section of the book until you've covered all the bases I laid out in the first section. Nothing!

The order of planning, saving, and investing are completely backward in this country. Americans are more concerned about funding their 401(k) plans and other retirement accounts than what's covered in any other chapter in this book. That's probably because it's the most advertised. If retirement is the *last* thing to happen in your financial life (short of dying), why is it the *first* thing you are funding? Does that make any sense?

I want you to build your castle the right way, and that means doing things in the right order, prioritizing the most important strategies that create the most efficiency. This way, you and your family will have a road map to get where you want to go with the best chance of positive outcomes and the most effective methods of risk management.

The order we will follow through this section of the book is:

1. Build and execute a budget so you know where your money is going … and where it *isn't* going.
2. Create margin by finding ways to live well while still saving.
3. Create liquidity in your life.
4. Look at your timeline of needs/wants and plan those purchases accordingly.
5. Utilize mortgages and home equity lines of credit (HELOC).
6. Utilize retirement accounts efficiently and effectively.
7. Uncover the common financial myths in your life and what to do to avoid the pitfalls associated with them.
8. Optimize employer matching and understand what to do with those funds after you leave.
9. Understand different investment strategies, how they are supposed to work, and how they can benefit you, including Turnkey Asset Management Programs (TAMP), Exchange Traded Funds (ETF), mutual funds, and fixed and variable annuities.

10. Factor in how to effectively integrate Social Security into your later years.
11. Discuss how to manage risk, the different types of risk, and how they affect you.
12. Introduce the concept of creating your own "retirement income plan."
13. Plan for life events.
14. Plan for living a long life and leaving a legacy of love to your family.
15. Consider alternative strategies for reaching your goals.

Building wealth isn't all that complicated, but it does take some time and effort. And it takes a commitment to making smart decisions over the long haul. If you're ready to take the first steps, I'm ready to show you where to go. We'll start in the following chapter...with your checkbook.

CHAPTER 14

NOTHING HAPPENS WITHOUT A BUDGET

*B*ACK IN 1959, WHEN VINCE LOMBARDI TOOK OVER THE fledgling Green Bay Packers as head coach, they were so bad that he finally threw up his hands, sat his team down and said, "Gentlemen, today we are going back to the basics of this game." Picking up a ball, he continued, "This is a football . . ." The rest is history.

In the world of personal finance, the "football," or the first brick of your financial castle, is the simple, basic monthly budget. It seems simple, but guess how many people don't do it.

How are you going to build wealth if you don't even know where your monthly income is going? No, I'm not talking about checking your online banking every week or two or using Excel spreadsheets. That only shows you where your money *went*. A budget, on the other hand, shows you where your money *is going*. That takes some planning.

Most people walking around today are totally addicted to the lifestyles they're trying so hard to maintain. Everywhere I look, I can see people spending a small fortune just to keep up appearances or keep up with where they think they *should* be at this point in their lives. At my age, and after spending a few decades helping people walk the financial tightrope, I can look back and identify two types of financial learning experiences peppered all throughout my own financial journey:

- **Life Tuition:** Times when I learned something important.
- **Stupid Tax:** Times when I didn't.

I've learned a lot from both, but I much prefer paying tuition than paying taxes!

Most of the stupid tax I've paid over my lifetime has revolved around lifestyle choices. I'm talking about buying cars when I couldn't afford them; getting new clothes when I didn't need them; paying bar tabs and restaurant bills when I was probably overdrawn in my checking account; and making minimum payments to credit cards when I got too far behind in paying them off every month. Those are just a few examples of the less-than-brilliant things I've done with my money. Trust me, the list goes on and on.

I even have a constant reminder of a bad decision in my home now. It's a beautiful antique armoire that serves as a place for glassware and a few bottles of adult beverages. It's had multiple uses in the thirty-plus years I've owned it. Soon after I bought it, I realized I shouldn't have. I vividly remember wondering how much I could sell it for to pay my electric bills!

And I've learned that you never *know* you're making a bad decision *while* you're making it. It's always a good decision . . . at the time. Otherwise, we would have chosen to do something else. But then . . . the moment of clarity strikes. It may be a day, a week, or a decade later, but we come face-to-face with a huge mistake. Maybe it's when the first bill comes for that big-ticket item that seemed like such a good purchase at the time. Maybe it's when you need to replace your roof, and you realize you shouldn't have spent all your savings on a Tesla. Maybe it's when you retire, and you realize you aren't quite as well-off as you expected to be.

A budget protects you from the bulk of these mistakes. How? Because it forces you to spend your money *on paper* before you spend it *for real*. It's an exercise in planning, control, and discipline. For all the power it wields in your life, though, a basic budget couldn't be simpler. It's really elementary. It's addition and subtraction, with some organization thrown in. That's it. You write your income at the top of the page, and then you subtract all the expenses you know you'll have for the month ahead. If you get to the bottom of the list and still have some money left over, congratulations! You've got some cushions for your castle. If you end up with a negative number—meaning you're planning on spending more than you're making—well, that makes you a pretty typical American. The problem is, the typical American is hurting financially. If you want to live in a castle, you've got to make a plan for building it. As drop-dead simple as it sounds, that plan is called a *budget*.

Set Up a System for Tracking Expenditures

We've lost sight of the basics when it comes to money. Whenever I ask simple questions to a prospective client or a friend who wants some advice, I am amazed at how inconsistent their answers have become. The first question I ask is, *What system do you use to track your spending, saving, and monthly outflows?* These days, people usually respond with, "I have online banking." Translation: they have no system other than the rearview mirror the bank provides.

For the last twenty-five years, as long as I've had a computer, I've been an advocate for Quicken financial software. It's kept me organized through a lot of financial decisions in my life. I always know where every dollar in my checking account comes from and where it goes. It even automates my reporting and tracks my spending in certain categories without me having to tinker with it too much. For example, my Quicken software knows when I've been at a Starbucks, and because of a parameter I set for it years ago, it automatically codes those transactions as a business expense because I'm almost always there meeting clients for discussions over coffee. This means it tracks every dollar I've spent at Starbucks and makes sure it shows up on my taxes as a business expense. All those cups of coffee add up, so that tax deduction comes in handy!

Know What You're Spending Your Money On

The second question I usually ask is, *If I asked you to tell me what you spent last year on [fill in the blank], could you tell me?* Most of the time, I get a blank stare. Let's test it with you.

How much have you spent on weekday lunches in the past year? How about gas? Groceries? Entertainment? Haircuts? Manicures? Clothes?

Were you guessing on your answer, or do you actually have a system of documentation that helped you figure it out? And were these *planned* expenses, or did you just pay for stuff as it came up and hoped there was enough money in your account to cover them? Or, even worse, did you just charge everything to a credit card and blindly pay the bill when the statement arrived each month?

Do you see the problem here? Your bank statement is the rearview mirror that shows you where you've been. Your budget is the windshield; it shows the road ahead of you. Your budget lets you anticipate the ups and downs, twists and turns, and caution signs of your financial journey. Without a budget, you're driving blind and praying you don't drive yourself and your family over a financial cliff.

On page 139 is a sample budget to use as a starting point. Remember, you cannot build a castle without a foundation, and your cash flow management is the foundation of any solid financial plan. Whether you use this form, make your own, or use one of the many great budgeting apps available like Quicken, YNAB (You Need a Budget), or Mint, you need a plan for your spending. Do something—even if you just scribble it down on a legal pad every month!

A Note for Dual-Income Couples

Bringing two lives together is one thing . . . but bringing two *incomes* together is something else entirely. If you married "for better or worse," it's probably best to combine your incomes into one budget. Separate accounts are fine, but everything needs to flow through one household budget first. Besides, it's all going to filter over to your 1040 tax returns anyway! As you can see, this is not complicated, but it is absolutely essential. This can be a challenge but once overcome, this simple strategy can help you, as a married couple, see where your hard-earned dollars are going and maybe find greater efficiencies of those dollars. Did I say vacation fund?

Monthly Budget

INCOME SOURCES	AMOUNT	
Paycheck 1		
Paycheck 2		
Paycheck 3		
Paycheck 4		
Other		
Other		
TOTAL INCOME		

EXPENSES	AMOUNT	
Savings		
Emergency Fund		
Retirement Accounts		
College Savings		
Other		
Other		
Other		

Giving		
Church		
Other		
Other		
Other		

Home Expenses		
Mortgage/Rent		
Mortgage 2		
Property Taxes		
Homeowner's Insurance		
Repairs		
Other		

Utilities		
Electric		
Gas		
Water		
Cable		
Internet		
Phone 1		
Phone 2		
Garbage		
Other		

Health and Medical		
Health Insurance		
HSA Contribution		
Prescription Drugs		
Life Insurance 1		
Life Insurance 2		
Other		

EXPENSES	AMOUNT	
Transportation		
Gasoline		
Oil Changes		
Car Payment 1		
Car Payment 2		
Auto Insurance		
Other		
Other		

Household		
Groceries		
Yard		
Housekeeping		
Hair and Beauty		
Clothing		
Furniture		
Pets		
Other		
Other		
Other		

Entertainment		
Restaurants		
Movies/Theatre		
Vacations		
Streaming Services		
Other		
Other		

Debt Payment		
Other		
Other		
Other		
Other		

Total Income		
<minus>		
TOTAL EXPENSES		
EQUALS		ZERO

CHAPTER 15

NEW JOB PAPERWORK: CHOOSING BENEFIT PLANS AT WORK

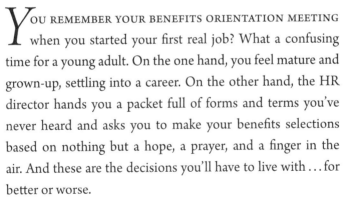

YOU REMEMBER YOUR BENEFITS ORIENTATION MEETING when you started your first real job? What a confusing time for a young adult. On the one hand, you feel mature and grown-up, settling into a career. On the other hand, the HR director hands you a packet full of forms and terms you've never heard and asks you to make your benefits selections based on nothing but a hope, a prayer, and a finger in the air. And these are the decisions you'll have to live with . . . for better or worse.

To my knowledge, they don't teach a class in college or trade school on how to manage money, choose an employee benefit plan(s), or balance a checkbook. Years ago, my nephew was thinking of joining me in my insurance and investment practice after college. I told him to take an introduction to insurance course and maybe an introduction to financial planning class with the elective hours he had remaining before graduation. Guess what? They weren't offered. This was at a major university and neither course was available? I was dumbfounded.

You've got a few places where you can look for advice: your parents (sometimes that's good, sometimes it's not); your friends (who probably don't know any more than you); the Internet (which has nine million competing systems, theories, and possibilities to sift through); and so on. How do we know who to trust?

I'm going to pick on my niece for this example, as I love her and she knows I enjoy picking on her. When she graduated college and got her first salaried job, she was given this huge PDF of information on the benefit package sponsored by her employer. It had to be at least sixty pages. Needless to say, she was slightly overwhelmed. Since HR directors have specific guidelines to follow—the most important is to not give benefit advice to an employee—she called her dad, my brother, who immediately told her to call her Uncle B (me). I told her to send it to me so I could review it for her. I have the required licensing to discuss these areas. Plus, I've done it for many of my clients over the years.

We started by looking at what her employer paid for, then what she could add as optional policies. They paid 100 percent of her health insurance and matched a portion of her contribution into the company 401(k) plan. They also gave her two times her salary in group life insurance. While I had her ear, I also asked her the basic questions from the first section of this book. Her auto insurance was in good order. Renters' insurance? Check. Bank account with a good tool for budgeting? Check, she used Mint.com. Payment plan established for repayment of student debt? Check.

So, here's what I recommended for her: a medical plan that had a reasonable deductible with doctor and prescription co-pays and group life insurance to pay off any debts she might otherwise leave to her parents. Dental was optional, so we calculated the annual cost to her; it equaled the price of two dental cleanings a year, so we didn't choose it. She was basically swapping dollars of premium versus benefit. I recommended she not choose the disability plan, only because it was expensive. Instead, she used those dollars for other means, such as setting up a systematic savings account from her checking account to get her savings and emergency fund started.

Finally, regarding the 401(k) plan, the employer match was fairly generous and was immediately vested, meaning she could take 100 percent of the match along with her contributions if she ever changed jobs. I told her to "max the match" and no more! Also, since the company offered a Roth 401(k) option, I encouraged her to choose that, and I recommended a specific type of mutual fund called a "lifestyle fund," which has all asset classes in it. This type of fund keeps investing simple and gives an optimum amount of investment diversification. It also takes the guesswork out of picking your own mutual funds when you have zero knowledge about them. I'll talk more about these things later.

She called me a few days later and told me the HR director was amazed at her selections and asked her how she came to the decisions she made. I can see her smile now as she told him and the other members of her recruiting class that her uncle was a financial advisor, and he had helped her. She also said everyone in her class chose the same options I recommended for her. Keep in mind that this story is intended for illustrative purposes. Your results will vary based on your personal needs and wants.

What is the takeaway for you, the reader, here? These are important decisions, and you need to know where to go for help. Unless you really know what you are doing, you could either overspend on benefits you *don't* need or fail to choose the benefits you *do* need. If you can, seek advice from a reliable source before you sign your benefits package, because each company's offerings are unique, and your needs are specific to you. The way to get the best building blocks for your castle and moat of protection is to have a professional advise you.

I wish I could sit down with you and personally walk you through each of these options, just like I did for my niece. Hey, if you're in Nashville, maybe I can! But for most of the people reading this, the best I can do is educate you on what most of those terms and options mean. I've done that on the insurance side already; now, let's get more familiar with the different investing options available to you.

CHAPTER 16

CASH (AND CASH EQUIVALENTS) ARE KING!

S AVING IS NOT SEXY. IT'S BORING. THERE'S NO ENDOR-
phin rush in setting money aside for future needs—
especially compared to that same endorphin rush when we
buy stuff. Even if we know we don't need it, it's still a rush.
Sometimes that makes it even more of a thrill!

According to the US Bureau of Economic Analysis, people
saved around 10–15 percent of their income in the 1970s. It plum-
meted to around 3 percent in the mid-2000s in the lead-up to the
Great Recession. In 2020, it was around 7 percent—less than half
of what my parents' generation saved.[9] Why do you think this is?
I have an idea—and it's probably not what you think. Sure, it's
easy to blame modern excess on all the entertainment and "toy"
options we have these days, but the truth is people have *always*
had plenty of excuses for spending money. What they *didn't* have
in the seventies, though, is interesting from a financial perspective. They did not have:

- Financial advisors
- Easy access to Individual Retirement Accounts (IRAs)
- Online trading platforms
- Easy access to information for mutual funds, individual stocks, and bonds
- 401(k) plans with their employer
- 529 college savings plans
- Health Savings Accounts (HSAs)
- Easy, abundant access to credit cards

You'd think these modern financial tools and products would make it easier for us to save more than our parents or grandparents did, but that's not the case.

So, what *did* they have? Mom and Dad had access to:

- Savings accounts
- Certificates of Deposit (CDs)
- Christmas clubs (ask your parents what these are)
- Layaway plans at department stores (ask about these too)
- Whole life insurance policies with guaranteed cash values
- Job stability that came from working at one company your entire career
- Company-sponsored pension plans with guaranteed retirement income and health care in retirement
- Discipline to not spend what they didn't have and to live within their means

Those things are mostly gone these days, and the few that remain are rarely explored. Today, per the Bureau of Labor Statistics, the median number of years that people have worked for their current employer is 4.1 years. To make this worse, the average tenure for millennials is 2.8 years. This means they will have ten to fifteen jobs over the course of their working lives![10]

Where does this shift leave us today? Overspending like crazy. I live in a Nashville neighborhood full of homes built in the sixties and seventies. I'm blessed to be where I am. My next-door neighbor just turned ninety-two, and she built her home in 1966! She's been there going on fifty-five years! If you go one mile to the east, you'll get to one of the wealthiest ZIP codes in Nashville with many, many multimillion-dollar homes. However, if you go one mile to the west, there's a cash advance or a check-cashing shop on every block. It's very telling.

I'm kind of in the middle . . . not too poor, not too rich. It's a nice, comfortable neighborhood that's similar to the Knoxville neighborhood I grew up in. Many of my neighbors are either retired and have lived in their homes for decades, or they are young families, just getting started in life. I'm constantly seeing parents with strollers walking in front of my home.

You know why some neighborhoods have so many payday lenders? It's because the people who live beyond their means and cannot afford their lifestyle take out these types of loans. Once you go down this path, it's hard to get yourself right side up. It's a slippery slope. Who knows, maybe they are also buying lottery tickets so they can hit it big and get rich quick. And the interest rates in those places are astronomical—some would argue they're illegal, but they are fully disclosed in very small print. But that's the price you pay for failing to save when you unexpectedly have a "life event." It's always the fine print that will come back to bite you, regardless of the situation.

Our savings rate as a nation is too low—historically around 5 percent on the high side, including our IRA and 401(k) contributions. I firmly believe in "world-class savings," which means putting 15–20 percent of your income away in various accounts annually. I'll show you how to do that in a later chapter.

As a country, we don't save unless we are given incentives to do so, such as tax-deductible contributions to retirement accounts or employer matching in 401(k) plans. Those are great options, and you should absolutely take advantage of them (we'll discuss these and other options later), but a 4 percent employer match shouldn't be the only thing that brings us to the savings table.

One "rule of thumb" I've heard from multiple sources, including the media and all the financial entertainers, is that you should have three to six months of income set aside for emergencies and other basic needs and expenditures. Given the extremely low interest rate environment we have experienced for the last decade, there is not a lot of motivation to put $10,000 or $20,000 in a savings account or money market that gets less than 1–2 percent annual return (if you're lucky). *But we've got to do it.* We must go back to that budget from the previous chapter and *create* the margin in our lifestyles to set money aside for those life events that creep up on us when we least expect it.

Cash and Cash Equivalents

What would happen if you had a car wreck like I had several years ago? Given what has happened with your health-care plan, do you have enough money available to meet your annual deductible and your maximum out-of-pocket expense? Maybe you should start there as an attainable amount. If you can't pull together the cash to meet your full health deductible on a moment's notice, you're just asking for trouble.

When life happens, the first things to look for are cash and cash equivalents. A *cash equivalent* is something that is *liquid*, meaning you can get the cash quickly. If you own a home, you could be eligible for a home equity line of credit (HELOC), which, if opened beforehand, can serve you well (if you treat it well). If you manage it correctly, money will be available when you need it most. If you use it for wild spending sprees or impulse purchases, you're defeating the purpose of having it *and* you'll find yourself deeper and deeper in debt. Credit cards are similar. They can be handy when used correctly, but a cash loan from a credit card is a *horrible* idea. The interest rate on cash advances is always much more than it would be on regular purchases. That fast cash will cost you big-time when the bill comes.

What about pulling out of your retirement accounts in an emergency? Isn't that fairly liquid? Well, yes and no. Yes, you can access the funds in your IRA before retirement, but making a premature withdrawal from an IRA is one of the worst financial decisions you could make. Pulling retirement funds out early to cover an emergency may seem like an easy answer in the short-term, but it'll come back to haunt you in the long run. Not only will you pay a 10 percent penalty for early withdrawal, but those dollars are tacked onto your taxable income, oftentimes resulting in paying taxes in a higher bracket than normal. Plus, you'll miss out on all the future earnings that withdrawal amount would have gained between now and retirement. If your retirement funds are in the company 401(k), you have to qualify for a specific hardship to access those funds. You can learn more about those in a document available to you called a "Summary Plan Description," which gives you all the information on your company retirement plan. Ask your HR director how to access this. Every retirement plan has one.

Taking money out of your 401(k) or IRAs early is called a *lost opportunity cost*, which I mentioned in the Moats section. It's what you would have earned had you not made the financial decision that forced the early withdrawal. It unplugs that money from the growth potential *and* it cuts your paycheck for months as you pay the loan back. It's a double whammy that doesn't look nearly as good a few months after the fact as it did in the heat of the moment. I've personally done this in my past, so I'm quite qualified to talk about it! It was an expensive lesson for me to learn, so trust me when I say it's always best to leave your retirement savings alone and never view your IRA or 401(k) as an emergency piggy bank.

Home Equity Lines of Credit, aka HELOCs

HELOCs are a great tool for a cash equivalent—if used properly, of course. They are also a great tool for debt management and reduction (again, only when used properly).

HELOCs became popular several decades ago. They were created so that a homeowner could borrow the equity in their home to make home improvements and/or additions. Say you want to add a new master bedroom or build a screened-in porch on the back of the house. You could pull money out of your home's value and pledge that equity as collateral. Today, HELOCs can be used for anything.

Here's a simple example of how the formula to qualify might look:

CURRENT HOME VALUE	$400,000
CURRENT MORTGAGE BALANCE	- 250,000
GROSS HOME EQUITY	= $150,000
PERCENTAGE AVAILABLE TO BORROW	80%
AMOUNT **AVAILABLE** TO BORROW	$120,000

You will quickly notice that I bolded the word "available." Just because it's available, doesn't mean you have to use it! All we are doing here is unlocking those available dollars. Why do I like these types of accounts? Simple. If you have a true financial emergency and don't have the required dollars to pay for that emergency, this could be a suitable alternative to taking premature withdrawals from your IRA or loans from your 401(k), going to a cash advance company, or taking cash advances from your credit cards—all of which are really bad ideas and do nothing but dig a deeper hole for people.

Why wouldn't you just use your credit card in an emergency? Out of curiosity, I just now pulled out one of my credit card statements to see what the cash advance interest rate was. It's a 25.24 percent variable rate! This is one of my travel cards that I use strictly to get airline miles for my new travel addiction.

When I am doing simple planning for my clients, oftentimes they have gotten themselves into credit card debt for a variety of reasons: retail therapy, change in income (but not in spending), true emergencies, and so on. Once someone has moved a balance from one card to another for that introductory zero percent interest rate, it rarely gets better. I've seen on multiple occasions where people are making minimum payments to keep the card active but most of that is going primarily to interest, not principal.

Compare that to a HELOC. One of the primary reasons I like HELOCs is the historically lower interest rates the bank charges. Maybe you've heard of the "fed funds rate"? This is the rate that banks pay to borrow money from the government. Typically, the bank will charge 1–2 percent above that rate. It's been as high as 6.51 percent in the fourth quarter of 2000 and, as of the time of this writing, it's around .08 percent.[11] HELOC interest used to be tax deductible, which made them even more attractive, but recent tax law changes did away with that.

Let's imagine I have a client with a credit card debt of $25,000, and the current interest rate on that card is 18 percent. That's $4,500 per year just in interest costs, which breaks down to $375 per month. They're not gaining ground in this scenario, especially if they have several other things on their financial wish list. If they were to qualify for a HELOC with a 4 percent variable rate and move their debt off the card and onto the HELOC, things would change dramatically. Instead of wasting $4,500 per year in interest, they'd only owe $1,000 per year in interest. If they kept that same $375/month payment, they'd be spending the same amount of money but knocking $3,500 per year off the principal balance. That's a winning strategy! This also gives them a stronger will to get rid of this balance, so they could really attack that balance if their plan allowed for it. There's something about hope that makes people work harder and do all they can to be better…like me on a treadmill, trying to get this aging body into shape so I can outlive my dad, who made it to ninety-one!

Many financial entertainers will disagree with me, saying "debt is debt." But if debt is a major stumbling block to gaining control over your money, and we can, with discipline, create a plan to get to a better place, why wouldn't we consider it?

In Summary

In the Moats section of this book, I talked about cash value life insurance as a tool for protecting your loved ones in the case of your death. Well, these are also great options for easy, penalty-free liquid cash in an emergency. You might think I'm still trying to sell the concept of cash value insurance (and maybe I am), but I've admitted to having certain biases in my professional life. This is one of them. Life insurance cash values are readily liquid via tax-free loan or withdrawal. It's a good tool when you need it most—and isn't that what insurance is all about? The financial entertainers say cash value life insurance is "a horrible investment." By definition, it's not an investment at all; but, if it's structured and used properly, it can be a great savings tool.

To recap, you can find cash and cash equivalents in:
- Savings accounts and money markets
- Home Equity Lines of Credit (HELOCs)
- Cash values in life insurance policies

Conversely, you do *not* want to pull cash from these places:
- Cash advances on credit cards
- Check cashing places, car title loans, or payday lenders
- Loans from 401(k) plans
- Premature withdrawals from IRA accounts

From the Carden Financial Archives

Now, let me tell you a personal story from the Carden archives about why all this is important. In 2013, I was not in a good cash position. I had recently paid the IRS for the prior year's taxes, paid two quarters of estimated taxes for the current year, funded my retirement accounts for the previous and current years, and had nothing left in my emergency fund. The market correction of 2008 reduced the market value of my condo, therefore reducing my equity. Things were … tight.

You know what would have been a crazy thing to do right then? Buy a house. And yet, that's exactly what I did. Out of nowhere, I got the bug to get out of my condominium and get back into a house. Amazingly, within a forty-eight-hour period, I found a home for sale that I fell in love with *and* I got a full-price cash offer on my condominium. And there I was, with no money to bring to the closing table on my new house.

But (there is always a "but," and this one is a good one) I had been overfunding my life insurance policy for years, meaning I was putting a significantly higher amount into the policy that was above and beyond what the stated premium was, and those dollars went directly into my cash value account, earning a tax-free rate much higher than what was available via money markets and savings accounts. I was systematically setting it aside because my budget allowed for it. The cash value grew at a reasonable rate and 100 percent tax-free. Have you ever noticed when you fill out a loan application, they ask for an itemized list of your assets and they always want to know what the life insurance cash values are? Can you guess why that matters to them?

The way I have always looked at it, from an asset allocation perspective, my *equity* allocation (meaning stocks and growth mutual funds) was in my Roth IRA and brokerage accounts. My *fixed* income allocation (safe money) was in my cash value account. Both of these are two of the very few *tax-free* strategies available today. If you see seminars and workshops on "tax-free investment strategies," most of the time they are talking about exactly these two items: Roth IRAs and over-funded cash value building life insurance policies.

When I met with my mortgage broker, I told her my story about being temporarily cash poor, but then I gave her my life insurance statement showing more than enough cash value available to go to closing. I think she was a little shocked when

I told her I had full access to 90 percent of that value within forty-eight hours—100 percent tax-free—via loan. The mortgage underwriter said in all her years, she had never seen someone use this strategy, but she easily approved my loan.

I made a phone call, filled out a form, and had a check in my hand soon thereafter. I basically borrowed the insurance company's money at a 6 percent annual rate of return, made the interest payment in advance, and paid off the loan within the next year. The money was returned to the company, my cash value account kept growing like normal all along, and I had my new home. Ta-da! The misnomer is that technically you don't borrow *your own* money. You borrow the *insurance company's* money via a policy loan, and its collateral is your cash value account.

If I had withdrawn money from my IRA, I would have paid taxes and a 10 percent penalty, *and* I would have lost all the future value of that IRA account. A life insurance loan, however, is a nonreportable event on my tax return because it's a loan! I paid it back in full, and the only out-of-pocket cost was the interest payment on the amount I borrowed.

It amazes me that the media always talks about *consumer spending*, but nobody ever talks about *consumer saving*. As I've said, it ain't sexy … but it sure is important.[12]

CHAPTER 17

WHERE DO YOU FIND THIS "SAVED" MONEY?

FOR THIS CHAPTER, WE'RE GOING TO LOOK AT YOUR budget. Remember, you shouldn't even be reading this chapter until you've completed your budget! One of the greatest feelings in the world is when you have margin working in your life. Margin to me is having the ability to not feel financially and emotionally squeezed by our life decisions. Margin gives us room to make better decisions with our money, our time, our emotions, and so many other areas of our lives. Regarding money, we can't find margin in your cash flow if we don't know where it's actually flowing.

When working with clients, there are a few places I look to find potential savings. After all, the less you're spending each month, the more room you can create for saving. The first place I check is their deductibles on auto, home, and health insurances. We talked about this a bit in the Moats section of the book, but let's review: The lower the deductible, the higher the annual premium. That means you're paying more each month/year for your insurance. What do you get for that extra money? If you have an accident and have to file a claim, you'll spend less out of pocket. Does that make sense to you? Because it doesn't to me! What we're saying here is that you're choosing to *definitely* spend more money today to avoid the *chance* of paying more money later. People jump into low-deductible plans without considering this basic fact. And, as a result, they usually end up paying far too much for their insurance than is necessary.

For example, say you've been carrying $100 comprehensive and $100 collision deductibles for the last ten years on your auto policy (meaning your out-of-pocket expense if you file a claim will only be $100), and the annual premium is $1,500. Let's assume you have not filed a claim for the entire ten-year period. Hypothetically, if you changed your deductibles to $1,000 comprehensive and $1,000 collision, the new premium might drop to around $900 per year. Guess what? We've just found $600 that comes back into your life. Multiply that amount by 10 years, and that's $6,000 of found money by one simple strategy. What could you do with those new dollars? Save or invest them? Purchase more protection to build a stronger moat? Pay off debt? Once you give it to an insurance company, in most cases, you never get it back!

Another place I look for potential savings is someone's entertainment and dining out budget. I get it. We all do it, we all enjoy it, and we are entitled to some fun after a hard week's work. But do you honestly have any idea how much you're spending on restaurants, bar tabs, movies, concerts, and coffee dates? If you've been living without a budget, my guess is this is going to be a major shock to you when you finally start tracking your expenses and planning ahead. Getting a handle on this can save you a ton of money, and I'm not saying you should stop going out and having fun. I'm just saying you should be smart about it.

For example, I love a good Kentucky bourbon. When I have a glass at a restaurant with dinner, I'm paying at a minimum $10–$17 for that glass of bourbon. However, when I have one at home with my friends, the entire *bottle* only costs me $30–$50. I can have a glass of bourbon every night for a couple of weeks for what I'd pay for just two drinks at a nice restaurant! It just doesn't make sense to pay ten times more for the privilege of drinking it in the restaurant or bar.

Another area of potential savings I see all the time is people's shopping budgets. Or, I guess I should say their shopping *expenses*, because there's usually no budget involved when someone's engaged in retail therapy. As I said in the beginning of this section, for many of us, spending money creates a huge endorphin rush. It's fun! The Amazon delivery person knows my front porch all too well! Unnecessary spending, though, will totally blow your budget, your financial plan, and your life if you're not careful. I have dear friends and clients—both men and women—who have full-blown addictions to buying shoes, purses, clothes, electronics, gadgets, and golf clubs. Can I get an amen?

Too many people complain that they simply don't have enough money to save anything for emergencies. You've got to want to change your habits before you start saving, and that's a challenge. I say this from experience. However, very rarely do I work with someone who *literally* can't find any margin at all to create some savings. By adjusting our habits, behaviors, and belief systems about how money works, and by truly embracing something as elementary as a working budget, we could be recapturing thousands of dollars a year.

So, now that we've *recaptured* those dollars that have been leaving our lives unnecessarily, how do we *redeploy* them? I'm glad you asked.

CHAPTER 18

TIMELINING YOUR SAVINGS

S O FAR, WE'VE BEEN TALKING ABOUT THE BORING SIDE
of savings—things like having cash on hand for emergencies and how to free up some cash flow in the monthly budget. Now it's time to kick things up a notch. This is where things at least *start* to get a little sexier.

I want to address three specific types of savings plans in this chapter: basic savings/investment accounts, Health Savings Accounts (HSAs), and 529 college savings plans. We'll start with the basics.

Basic Savings: Lining Up Your Dominoes

Imagine a row of dominoes lined up, ready to fall one after the other. This is a good way to picture your savings and investment strategies.

What's the first financial domino that will fall? Simple: it's the short-term needs that could occur within the next year or two, which might include deductibles for insurance claims, car maintenance, vacations, and gifts. How much money should you set aside for this area? $1,000, $5,000, $10,000? More? The amount is different for everyone depending on what your plans are over the next couple of years. You'll be able to determine this by looking at your budget and planning for upcoming expenses.

Whatever amount you decide is appropriate for your situation, you need to keep it liquid and readily accessible. This is money that you usually need quickly as situations arise, so you don't want it tied up in complicated, long-term investments. If you're raiding your 401(k) to pay for a new set of tires, you're doing it wrong!

There are three words that I want you to apply to every dollar in this part of the book: *use, enjoyment,* and *control.* That is, in the face of a financial need or as a part of your financial plan, can you *use* that dollar? Can you *enjoy* that dollar? Do you have *control* over that dollar?

Set up either a savings account at a bank or credit union or an investment account with a money market fund, then protect that account in the case of your death. If you're single, you can get an individual brokerage account with a Transfer on Death (TOD) designation. If you're married or cohabitating with a significant other, have your financial advisor establish a Joint Tenant with Rights of Survivorship (JTWROS). Both the TOD and JTWROS will help transfer monies at your death and aid in avoiding the hassles of dealing with probate. JTWROS ensures the survivor inherits the account with no adverse tax or probate consequences. TOD is for people like me who have no spouse. If you have children and are divorced, this is where your kids are named as beneficiaries. In my case, having no natural children, I've named my niece and nephew as beneficiaries on my accounts. (Courtney, you get $1.00. Chase, you get $1.50.)

Now, what's the second domino that will fall? Think about the things that are maybe two to five years out. If you just had your first child, day care and things like private school meet that time frame. You can work with an advisor to help match your money to your time frame and see how aggressive you need to be in saving or how aggressive your savings plans need to be in terms of risk/reward. If your car is already a decade old with 100,000 miles, it's reasonable to assume you'll need a new one in the next five years. If you're on year seventeen of a twenty-year roof, you'll probably need to put a new roof on the house in this time frame. Again, these things are not surprises and should not be considered emergencies. You know these things are coming, so plan for them.

The third domino represents things that are five to ten years out, the fourth domino is ten to fifteen years out, and so on. If you imagine yourself *funding* each domino, how much would each one need? Honestly, I can't tell you. That's for you and your advisor to map out. My point here is to simply convince you to match your savings/investments to your future needs. That's called *timelining your savings*, and it ensures you've got the cash on hand to handle life's expenses as they come up.

Health Savings Accounts

While you can use basic savings and investing accounts for a variety of purposes, other investing products are deemed *single use assets*, meaning they are designed for only one purpose. This is where the Health Savings Account (HSA) falls. I love the HSA. They're awesome, and when I could have one based on the type of health plan I had, I did.

If you have a qualifying high-deductible health plan (HDHP), you can open an HSA. This is a special type of savings account at a financial institution designed specifically for health-related expenses. The HDHP and the HSA were created to give people incentives to elect higher deductibles to reduce the utilization of their health-care plan, and theoretically, reduce the annual costs. The beauty is that your contributions into the account are 100 percent tax-deductible up to the max contribution limit for that year. In 2021, as I write this, the government allows you to contribute $3,600 annually as an individual and $7,200 as a family. Plus, if you're over fifty-five like me, you can add an additional $1,000 to the account regardless of marital status.[13] I guess the government thinks old guys like me will have more health expenses than younger folks. Hey, that's fine with me. I'll take any tax-deductible opportunity to save that I can get! They also carry forward to the future years so the account can increase significantly over time.

The really cool part is that you can deduct the contribution *and* withdraw it for a qualified medical expense in the same year—or even in the same month! As long as the money flows into the HSA and is paid out of the HSA to the provider, you can write it off on your taxes. You can also use those tax-deductible dollars to pay for long-term care premiums later in life. It's a great option if you have a high-deductible health-care plan. Again, your broker will be able to direct you to the best options, so be sure to ask about the HSA.

529 Plans: Planning for College

529 college saving plans have become enormously popular in the last decade. These provide a tax-favored way to save for your child's college expenses in a variety of mutual funds with several well-known money managers, such as American Funds, Vanguard, TIAA, and Fidelity.

These plans used to be only for eligible educational institutions such as any college, university, vocational school, or other postsecondary educational institution eligible to participate in a student aid program administered by the US Department of Education. However, with the 2017 tax law change, they are now eligible for elementary or secondary school tuition, books, and even computers needed for classwork.

The 529 is a great tool for your children's education—especially for elementary or secondary school expenses. Your contributions are made in the name of a child or a grandchild, and the funds are intended to be used only for *that* child. The contributions grow tax-deferred and, if used correctly for eligible expenses, the withdrawals are 100 percent tax-free. That's right: this is one of the government's rare tax-free growth opportunities, and I'll take advantage of them every chance I can get.

One idea I always mention to parents when we establish 529 plans is that they send the information on the newly established plan to the child's grandparents, aunts, uncles, and so on. That way, others have the chance to contribute to the college savings plan on Christmases, birthdays, baptisms, graduations, and other gift-giving events. How much money do loving friends and relatives spend on unnecessary toys every year that end up buried at the bottom of the child's closet? Sending that cash to a 529 instead creates an exponential bang for their buck, and it helps ensure the child has money when they need it the most.

This takes a new mindset, however—or should I say it takes an *old* mindset? When I was very young, I remember my grandparents giving me twenty-five dollars in US savings bonds every Christmas and birthday. Contributing to a 529 can create that same sense of nostalgia, and it's a great way for a grandparent to give a gift that might very well outlast them.

The cost of college is insane, and far too many students are graduating school and entering the workforce already with tens of thousands of dollars of debt. I remember attending my niece and nephew's graduation ceremonies at the University of Tennessee. About one thousand students walked in each graduation. According to NerdWallet's extensive 2020 household debt study, bachelor's degree recipients leave school with an average student loan debt of $28,950.[14] That means by attending two graduation ceremonies, I saw more than $57 million in debt walk across the stage—and that doesn't count the debt some of them will keep racking up as they enter graduate programs.

I have a good friend who graduated from medical school at Vanderbilt University. His student loans total over $250,000! Fortunately, he's now getting into private practice and making well into six figures...but still, a quarter million in debt before you even start your career? Geez. And how many young adults are getting out of college or graduate school with no job offers on the table? Can you imagine finally finishing multiple degrees and trying to figure out how to pay off a six-figure student loan while working at Starbucks? It's a devastating problem, one the next generation will be dealing with for literally decades to come.

If you are a parent, passionate about your children going to college, and are reasonably sure they will, the 529 plan is the way to go. If you are not sure if your children will go to college, then maybe a regular investment account is better. That way, you'll still get some growth, but you'll lose the special tax benefits of the 529. Either way, keep your dominoes in mind. And, if you do save in a 529 but your child decides not to go to college, the money can be transferred to another family member's 529 plan without a penalty, or you can cash it out and take the financial hit.

Depending on your age, you might be facing both your child's college education and your retirement *at the same time*, and you'll have to choose which is more important. It's a difficult conversation to have with my clients. Hopefully, you'll have planned for each separately. If your kids are still young, you still have time!

There's Always a Catch

Fair warning: HSA and 529 plans come with a catch. Big surprise, since the government created them. With most government programs, the catch is hidden in the details and usually hits you on the back end of the transaction. That's definitely true here.

You will notice I used the term *eligible expenses* in explaining both the HSA and the 529. The HSA contribution is tax-deductible, but the withdrawal is tax-free only if it's used for *qualified medical expenses*—and the government sets the rules for what qualifies. If you use money in your HSA for nonmedical expenses, the contribution becomes taxable *and* you'll get hit with a 20 percent penalty (if you're under age sixty-five).

The 529 plan contribution is not tax-deductible, but the withdrawal is tax-free if it's used for *qualified education expenses*. Again, the government defines what qualifies. If I use 529 funds for noneducation expenses—such as a new roof or a vacation—any gains in the plan are taxable and subject to a 10 percent penalty. This has happened to some of my clients who have funded 529 plans for their grandchildren, only to learn that while the first three took advantage of Granddad's gift, the other two have no desire whatsoever to continue past high school graduation.

See why we call them *single-use assets*? You have to use them for their intended purpose, or you'll pay a penalty. Of course, you could skip the HSA and 529 and save for your dominoes in a regular investment account. You'll miss out on the tax advantages of these plans, meaning you'll ultimately pay more in taxes on your growth, but you'll also avoid the penalties if you need to use the money for something else. There are pros and cons whichever way you go, but if you know you're going to have some medical expenses (and you will) and you know your child is going to college someday, these two types of accounts work beautifully for their intended purposes. But only if they're managed correctly, and only if you've completed the previous steps I've outlined so far in this book.

CHAPTER 19

MORTGAGES: FUNDING THE CASTLE YOU LIVE IN

*I*THINK HOMEOWNERSHIP IS ONE OF THE GREATEST BENE-fits offered in our country. Amazingly, I meet people in their fifties and sixties who have chosen to rent their home their entire adult lives, only to find out the home they could have purchased for $50,000 is now worth over $500,000. Now they're totally dependent on whether their landlord chooses to sell their home out from under them.

One of my clients passed away a few years ago. He was a songwriter/musician. He wrote one major hit song many years ago that was performed and recorded by one of the biggest names in music. Basically, he lived off the royalties from that song his entire career. He told me that the smartest thing he ever did was listen to his manager, who told him to take some of those royalties and buy a home, and to buy it in a specific neighborhood. He probably paid less than $100,000 for it, but at the time of his death, it was worth over $700,000. Buying a home is a shrewd investment strategy, but most people will need a mortgage in order to make it happen.

For simplicity's sake, there are three types of mortgages: thirty-year fixed, fifteen-year fixed, and adjustable rate. The most popular is the thirty-year fixed because, in most cases, the monthly payment is lower. The fifteen-year fixed usually has a lower interest rate, but the monthly payment is higher because it's designed to pay off in fifteen years. The adjustable-rate mortgage has its place, and I have used them personally. When I bought my first home, I knew I wasn't going to stay there for a long period of time, and the adjustable-rate plan allowed me to spend less to buy the house I wanted then. My home today is my "forever home," so my strategy is different.

The Thirty-Year Mortgage

This type of loan enables a person to purchase the home they want with the least amount of monthly expense. I recommend putting less down on a home to avoid locking up a large amount of money into the home that you could use more efficiently in your financial plan in other areas (think 529 for college, 401(k) for retirement, bolstering your insurance plans, and so on).

The Fifteen-Year Mortgage

Financial entertainers recommend a fifteen-year mortgage for their readers, listeners, and watchers, as it continues their theme of debt avoidance. Someone with this mortgage will pay a higher payment each month but have a lower interest rate, and their home will be completely paid for in fifteen years. It sounds nice, but let me give you some examples of reasons I don't prefer this mortgage.

Take my grandfather, who built his family home in the late 1940s. Granddad was a child of the Great Depression and remembered that, in those years, the bank could "confiscate" your home if you didn't have the means to make the monthly payments. At the time, he had a nice portfolio of blue-chip stocks that he sold in order to own his home outright. This is his *lost opportunity cost*: the cost of paying off his mortgage versus keeping those stocks throughout his life and even passing them down to his family. There's no telling what that asset could be worth today. I refer to Granddad's strategy as "Depression Era Thought." It worked for him ... or did it?

Or consider the client who finds the idea of "no house payment" appealing but hasn't thought through their long-term plans. Maybe they're planning to move to Florida when they retire, or maybe they'd move closer to their children if their spouse died. Why would they want to put all their money in the house, knowing that it will only be worth what someone is willing to pay on the day they want to sell it?

Finally, remember that in the last five years we have seen historically low mortgage interest rates. If you've been in your home for five years and own a thirty-year mortgage, then you only have twenty-five years left to pay it off. Once you refinance you might qualify for a lower interest rate and lower monthly mortgage, but you're starting a brand-new thirty-year clock on a brand-new mortgage. Assuming you refinance every five years, you will be restarting that clock over and over again. If your plan is to truly be mortgage debt–free, then structure your mortgages accordingly.

Ever wonder why the fifteen-year mortgage rate is less than the thirty-year? It has to do with *velocity of money*, meaning how many times you can use a dollar. If you've got $10,000 in a savings account, a bank can loan those dollars out multiple times. You're getting 1–2 percent on your deposit, and they are getting no telling how much by loaning out your $10,000 to their other customers.

This is called the *Fractional Reserve System*, in which only a fraction of bank deposits is backed by actual cash on hand and available for withdrawal. Google it. With a fifteen-year mortgage, the lower interest rate is an incentive for you to pay their money back sooner, so they can loan it out faster. Ever wonder how the biggest and nicest buildings in every city and town are banks?

Adjustable-Rate Mortgages

Now, let's talk about adjustable-rate mortgages, in which the interest rate is only guaranteed for a specific period of time like one, three, five, or ten years. I most often see these used when someone knows exactly how long they are going to stay in a certain home. Adjustable-rate percentages have historically made qualifying for the loan more financially feasible— meaning it's a way for people who really can't afford to buy a house to buy a house.

It's hard for me to not point out that these types of loans were one of the primary reasons for the financial failure of 2007–2009. The lending industry had created a specific adjustable-rate mortgage called *negative amortization*. I owned one of these and, on a whiteboard, they worked beautifully. I knew what I was doing, but the majority of people who bought this type of mortgage did not. Fundamentally, they worked much like how your credit card works. There's the minimum payment, the recommended payment, and the payment to pay the loan off in a specified number of years—normally fifteen or thirty, since they were mortgages. Most of the people who used that loan bought more home than they should have because they only planned to make that minimum payment.

This is where things got ugly. Typically, a person qualifies for a loan based on current and former income, assets and liabilities, available down payment, and the ability to make the monthly payment. This is called a *prime-rate mortgage* and is the standard today.

A different type of loan used then was the *NINJA loan*—an acronym for "no income, no job, no assets." People bought homes with no income, no job, and no assets . . . based on the minimum monthly payment schedule that was initially disclosed to them.

But these were *adjustable-rate* mortgages! Yeah. So, these NINJAs bought homes based on the minimum payment they saw at closing, and before long, they received a new statement from the mortgage company with an adjusted (much higher) rate. They couldn't afford the payments, so they simply walked away from the home. In some cities, this happened by the thousands, which led to the collapse in the market during that time.

There are a lot of financial myths in the area of home ownership and mortgages, many of which are driven by the personal biases of your favorite financial entertainers. *En masse*, their advice may work. The thing is, though, you don't buy a home *en masse*. Your situation is *your situation*. You can't make all your financial decisions based on what works for the average person; you have to tailor your decisions to your specific situation. Working with a true mortgage professional will benefit you greatly. Yes, there could be lower rates via the Internet, but just like a good financial advisor can help you make good decisions on your savings and investment planning, the same applies for a good mortgage professional. In the end, the advice that sounds great on an advertisement may be terrible for you. So dig into this stuff, talk to your advisor, and identify the plan that works best for you.

CHAPTER 20

TAKE THE MONEY AND RUN: UTILIZING RETIREMENT ACCOUNTS AND EMPLOYER MATCHING

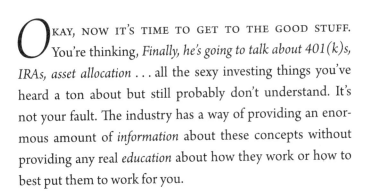

O KAY, NOW IT'S TIME TO GET TO THE GOOD STUFF. You're thinking, *Finally, he's going to talk about 401(k)s, IRAs, asset allocation . . .* all the sexy investing things you've heard a ton about but still probably don't understand. It's not your fault. The industry has a way of providing an enormous amount of *information* about these concepts without providing any real *education* about how they work or how to best put them to work for you.

First Things First

Now, as we get started, I want you to think back to that row of dominoes I told you to imagine in chapter 18. See that domino near the very back? The one toward the end of the row? That's the retirement domino. Short of death, it's one of the last dominoes to fall. However, you would be dumbfounded at the number of people who will completely blow off the first nineteen chapters of this book in their personal and financial lives and go straight to retirement!

Part of the problem is the greed our society inspires. It's like we've been groomed to become addicted to a set of retirement and investment drugs, including:

- The drug of the stock market
- The drug of the employer match
- The drug of tax deferral
- The drug of retiring in a lower tax bracket (which is a fallacy)

I consider all these drugs to be highly addictive and potentially destructive.

Another part of the problem is my generation, the baby boomers, telling their kids, "Start early and fund [fill in the blank] to the max! That's what I would have done if I had a plan like this when I was your age!" Yeah, right.

I have thirty-year-old clients with $100,000 in their retirement accounts. It's impressive, I must admit. Then they tell me their dream is to open their own business in the next three to five years. See the disconnect? Their retirement account is for *retirement*, not for opening a business in their mid-thirties Not only can they not use that money to open a business, but they can't even use it to secure a bank loan. Many clients are shocked to learn they cannot collateralize an IRA in any way, shape, or form.

My rule for how younger people should manage their retirement plan contributions is this: until they are fully protected against life-changing events and have become world-class savers, retirement should be the last thing on their minds. Given the government's periodic increasing amount of annual contribution into 401(k) plans, plus the catch-up provisions (extra contributions you're allowed to make in the years leading up to retirement) beginning at age fifty, you can grow your retirement accounts significantly with a disciplined approach after you've accomplished your other goals. When you get to the point in your life where you can focus on accumulating wealth for retirement, this is when you need to be as assertive as you possibly can in growing those retirement and investment accounts in the most prudent way possible. Once you get to this point, then you can begin to visualize those "golden years" from all of the television advertisements.

The government has realized that many Americans have not saved enough for retirement, so they have created the "catch-up provisions" for both IRAs and 401(k) plans. I'll talk about this in a few paragraphs. This is a great benefit for many Americans if they have created the financial ability to take advantage of these provisions.

If I'm working with a younger client who is craving the drug of the stock market and absolutely *must* take advantage of the drug of the employer 401(k) match, I ask that they at least meet me in the middle. My advice for those who are dead set on jumping into the market right out of the gate:

max your contributions up to the employer match—but no more! Some companies don't match at all. Some match on a percentage basis. Some match in company stock. Some match on a "years of service" schedule. Whatever your employer offers, if you feel like you have to do it, take up to the match and then focus on all the other things we've discussed in this book so far. Otherwise, you'll be building your castle with no moat or foundation to protect it!

Understanding the Drug of Tax Deferral

IRAs, 401(k)s, 403(b)s, SEP IRAs, and 457 plans are all examples of what are called *qualified plan assets*. And who "qualifies" it? The US government! That means they set the rules for how taxes are handled, how much you can contribute, and what happens to the money upon distribution in these types of investments. I know all these letters and numbers can get confusing, but it's actually pretty simple. Whenever you see something with a three-digit number and maybe a letter at the end, those refer to sections of the Internal Revenue Service tax code that define those plans. For example, a 401(k) is a retirement plan that is specified under section 401, subsection (k) of the tax code. An IRA is a rare retirement plan that goes by its name instead of its number; technically it's a 408 plan because it is laid out in section 408 of the tax code.

So why is the tax treatment such a big deal? Well, let me ask you a question: *if you were a farmer, would you want to pay tax on the seed ... or on the harvest?*

Read that again! Obviously, the tax on the seed is much smaller than the tax on the entire harvest. That's why it is important to understand the benefits of the Roth 401(k) and the Roth IRA and why they could be the best options for you, especially as you focus on retirement income planning.

"Roth" refers to a special kind of IRA or 401(k) plan in which you invest *after-tax* dollars—meaning your contributions *into* the plan are taxed at your normal tax rate, but the investment that grows is 100 percent *tax-free*. So, when you start taking distributions from the Roth account in retirement, you'll pay zero in taxes. That's what I meant by taxing the seed or the harvest. In this example, the money you contribute is the *seed*, and the growth you accumulate over the life of the account is the *harvest*.

The Roth 401(k) Option

A common misnomer is that the word *Roth* is strictly for IRAs. Not true! Many 401(k) plans now have a Roth option, so check your benefits Summary Plan Description. If you have one available, you can fund up to $19,500 annually, plus an additional $6,500 via catch-up provision at age fifty for a total contribution of $26,000 annually.[15] Many companies (but not all) offer a Roth 401(k) option alongside the traditional 401(k), yet very few employees are aware of it. Conversely, those companies that still don't offer the Roth 401(k) option make me scratch my head.

The Roth IRA Option

While the Roth IRA is a great savings vehicle for retirement, not everyone qualifies for it. For the tax year 2021 (and this is subject to change on an annual basis), if either you or your spouse is covered by a qualified retirement plan through your employer and make more than $125,000 as a single filer or $198,000 married filing jointly, you're either subject to a reduced contribution limit or completely ineligible. And if you do qualify, you are limited to a max contribution limit each year ($6,000 per person as of 2021). If you're over age fifty, you can kick in an extra $1,000 per year. These contribution limits are subject to change annually, so either make Google your friend, or, better yet, hire a CPA and/or financial planner to help you figure it out.

Here's a plus: depending on your income, you could qualify to fund both your company 401(k) plan *and* a Roth IRA. This is where your advisor and CPA become invaluable interpreting your personal income situations and determining eligibilities and contribution amounts. Sometimes, the fine print can be your friend!

Traditional vs. Roth IRA

I'm obviously a fan of the Roth, but don't just take my word for it. Let's put a traditional IRA and a Roth IRA head-to-head and see which comes out on top. Proponents of the traditional IRA, high on the drug of tax deferral, will tout the benefits of its tax-deferred status. Basically, *tax-deferred* means that you don't pay the taxes on the money you contribute today (the seed), and instead, you'll defer the taxes until you make withdrawals on the growth (the harvest) at retirement. This lets you contribute more because you aren't burdened by having to pay any money in taxes up front. Then by retirement, they say, you'll probably be at a lower tax bracket anyway. It's a decent argument...but is it really so cut-and-dried?

Let's focus on a single year's contribution for the sake of simplicity. I'm using my trusty HP-12C financial calculator here. Let's say you're thirty-five years old, you're in a 20 percent tax bracket, and you have $5,000 (present value or PV) to invest into a retirement account. After thirty years with an average rate of return of 6 percent, the future value(FV) of your $5,000 investment is $28,717.

$$\$5,000PV \times 30 \text{ years} \times 6\% = \$28,717 \text{ FV(pre-tax)}$$

At age sixty-five—still in the same 20 percent tax bracket—you decide to pull that exact amount out of your retirement account to buy a new car. What will the taxes look like?

Using the same exact calculation as before, if you invested in a traditional IRA, you got to deduct that $5,000 investment from your taxes the year you invested it. At your 20 percent tax bracket, that means you avoided $1,000 in taxes that year. Great! However, when you pull that $28,717 out at age sixty-five, you have to pay the taxes on the full withdrawal amount. At the same 20 percent tax bracket, that means you'll owe $5,743 in taxes when you pull the money out.

$$\$28,717 \times 20\% \text{ taxes} = \$5,743 \text{ due to the government}$$

But what if you had invested your $5,000 in a Roth IRA instead? Well, you would have put $5,000 into the retirement account, same as before. Only this time, you can't deduct the contribution on your tax return, so you pay the income taxes now (on the seed). At the 20 percent tax bracket, that means you'll pay the $1,000 in taxes that you would have avoided with a traditional IRA. However, things look a bit different when you pull the $28,717 out at age sixty-five. The Roth grows tax-free, remember? That means when you make that withdrawal, you'll owe *nothing* in taxes. Zip. Nada. None. Instead of paying $5,743 in taxes, like you would have done at age sixty-five with a traditional IRA, you only paid $1,000 in taxes at age thirty-five, when you put the money into the account.

$$\$5,000 \times 30 \text{ years} \times 6\% = \$28,717 \text{ tax-free}$$

See how the drug of tax deferral works against you? But wait, it could be even worse than that. What happens if income tax brackets *rise,* and you find yourself in a 40 percent tax bracket at retirement? The traditional IRA requires you to pay the tax upon distribution no matter the current rate. The Roth, on the other hand, is still 100 percent tax-free.

The "Lower Tax Bracket" Fallacy

If you are truly addicted to the drug of tax deferral, then the traditional IRA example described here may not have convinced you to go with the Roth instead of a tax-deferred option—especially if you believe you'll likely retire in a lower tax bracket than you were in during your working years. That's why I also want to show you two more separate but important facts.

The chart below shows a history of the US Marginal Tax Rates.[16] These are the highest "marginal" brackets.

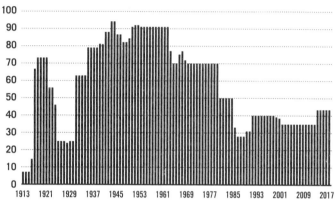

History of the US Marginal Tax Rates 1913–2017

Key periods over the past century reflect the following top marginal tax rates:

- World War I: 75 percent
- Great Depression: 25 percent
- World War II: 94 percent
- Reagan Era: 35 percent
- Current: 37 percent
- Tomorrow: Who knows?

Let's say you have funded your 401(k) plan from the Reagan Era to today, the lowest *consistent* tax brackets in our history. What happens to your strategy of long-term tax deferral if the income brackets go back to where they were in the sixties and seventies? I mean, even with the general consistency of the brackets over the past forty years, the top bracket has still seen an eleven-point increase since the early eighties. When you choose tax-deferred plans *over* the tax-free Roth, you're basically making a bet that the market will be right where you want it twenty or forty years from now. That's a pretty big bet!

Considering the continued economic and warfare threats we're constantly facing abroad—not to mention the growing political divide here at home—I have no idea where our national economy will be in the next forty years. We could be sitting on all-time low tax brackets, or we could be squashed beneath all-time high tax brackets. There's just no sure way to know. The one thing I *do* know is that I'd rather take a little tax hit today if it means getting tax-free income during my retirement years.

But what happens if the tax brackets remain largely the same? Let's assume your retirement accounts did great over time and your total retirement income (including Social Security) is equal to the income you earned throughout the last decade of your working years. Does that mean you'll stay in the same tax bracket—20 percent, for example—in retirement? Not necessarily.

When you're younger and working, you have tax advantages working in your favor, helping you stay in a lower tax bracket. For example, you might have tax-deductible mortgage interest, tax-deductible retirement plan contributions, and child tax credits for having dependent children living at home, among other deductions. If you are still able to itemize your deductions, that, too, could create tax savings.

However, there's a good chance you might not have these deductions in retirement. If you've paid your house off, raised the kids, and are taking withdrawals from that tax-deferred retirement account, those three major tax deductions are no longer available. And if your tax deductions disappear while your retirement income equals what you were making while working, guess what? By default, even if tax brackets never change, you could theoretically find yourself in a higher marginal tax bracket in retirement . . . totally dispelling the myth of retiring in a lower tax bracket.

Am I saying that funding retirement accounts is a bad thing? No! What I am saying is that retirement is one of the last dominoes to fall in your financial life, so prioritize it accordingly. If you're fifty years old, and your college funding plans are complete, your short- and intermediate-term accounts are plentiful, your career path is secure, and you see clear skies ahead toward your retirement, now you can go for it and fund them to the max. If you are maintaining world-class savings of 15–20 percent (or even higher), your financial plan is working for you. Remember, this account is only funding a part of the rest of your life.

You *Can* Take It with You

The last point I want to make here is that, contrary to popular belief, when it comes to company retirement plans, you *can* take it with you. No, I'm not saying you can take your sports car and jet ski through the pearly gates when you die! I'm saying you can take your company-sponsored retirement plans with you when you leave the company.

One of the most common financial mistakes I see people make is leaving their 401(k) with their former employers after they change jobs. I've met with clients who literally had six or more different 401(k) accounts scattered across the country as a type of financial travel log of their former jobs. Regardless of why it was done, this is a huge mistake, and it could result in an inefficient asset allocation strategy as well as a failure to optimize the growth of those accounts.

When you put money into a 401(k), your contribution dollars are vested immediately. If you get a company match, the employer's contributions into your account may not vest immediately depending on their vesting schedule. However, after six years in most plans, the company's contributions are also 100 percent vested. That means all the money in those accounts is *yours*—not the company's. It's your account, and you get to decide what to do with it.

While you technically *can* cash it out, you should never do this for the reasons I've already discussed. Instead, you have two real options: roll these dollars directly into an IRA or transfer them directly into your new company's 401(k) plan. With the IRA rollover, you have infinite investment strategies. That is, you aren't limited to the handful of funds that are available in a company's 401(k) plan. Instead, you get to choose from a world of investments and investment strategies on the open market. I will discuss these in a later chapter.

In addition, all management fees, broker fees or commissions, and so on are fully disclosed, so you know exactly what you are being charged. Plus, if you're using an advisor, hopefully he or she is actually *advising* you, meaning you're getting financial advice from a duly licensed financial professional.

If you roll the funds into your new company's 401(k) plan, you preserve the tax deferral and might think you're beating the system. In reality, though, the system is working against you. First off, even though you don't see them, administration fees and other ancillary costs of running the plan are netted out of your returns. Second, most plans have no advisor affiliated with them to help you make the best decisions. Third, and probably most importantly, you are limited to the investment choices provided by that company's 401(k) plan.

Once again, here is where the advice and counsel of a competent financial advisor can make a significant difference in your financial future!

CHAPTER 21

CHASING INVESTMENT RETURNS AND MODERN PORTFOLIO THEORY

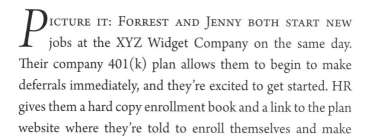

*P*ICTURE IT: FORREST AND JENNY BOTH START NEW jobs at the XYZ Widget Company on the same day. Their company 401(k) plan allows them to begin to make deferrals immediately, and they're excited to get started. HR gives them a hard copy enrollment book and a link to the plan website where they're told to enroll themselves and make their investment decisions.

That night, they pour through all the information and are surprised to see more than forty options in the company plan. That's great! Except . . . neither Forrest nor Jenny is a financial expert. They're both in their late twenties and have heard that they need to take advantage of retirement saving early, but they're clueless on what they should do. They've heard the financial entertainers talk about picking funds with good long-term track records, so they choose a handful of funds with the best five-, ten-, and fifteen-year average returns. Basically, they're throwing darts blindfolded and hoping one hits a bullseye. But what else can they do? They have no other advice available to them. It's another SWAG situation—a *Scientific Wild @$$ Guess*.

Do those chosen options match their risk tolerances? What if Jenny is comfortable with moderate risk but Forrest is more conservative? If they are chasing returns, they are likely putting themselves into aggressive investment options, but they may not even know it. And those of us who survived the double-digit negative returns of 2008 realize what these young investors may not: enough time has passed since that market correction that it doesn't factor into a fund's ten-year history anymore. That's a huge omission for any fund's recent historical returns! However, they pick their funds and take their chances, hoping for a good outcome.

It's like Forrest's mother always told him: "Stupid is as stupid does." Or was it "Run, Forrest, run"?

Average versus Actual Returns

These two terms often get confused, but hopefully as I go through the following example, you will begin to see how different they are. Actual return is the actual gain or loss an investor experiences on an investment or in a portfolio in a given period of time. Typically, this is illustrated on a year-by-year basis. Average return is the total annual returns added together and then divided by a period of years, such as five, ten, or fifteen years. It's quite common for people to look at the average annual returns when making their investment selections inside their 401(k). What I want to do now is give an example of how this could be misleading. This is basic math, and when someone first showed this to me years ago, I was blown away. Today I use this example with all of my investment and planning clients.

Let's say you come to me with a pile of cash to invest and you aren't sure what to do with it. Maybe your lucky numbers finally hit on the lottery, and you won $100,000. Or maybe good ol' Aunt Sally recently passed and left you $100,000. I immediately go to work using every piece of knowledge and experience available to me, such as risk tolerance questionnaires, time frame of the investment, liquidity needs, and so on—all the things a prudent advisor must do for his clients.

I know I'm using an extreme example here ($100,000 rarely falls from the heavens), but I have a big point to make and $100,000 is a nice round number. Here's how it plays out for the next four years in our made-up scenario:

- **Year 1:** You get a 100 percent rate of return, leaving you with $200,000 in your account. Boom!
- **Year 2:** Things go south, and you end up with a 50 percent *loss* for the year, bringing your account back down to $100,000.
- **Year 3:** Lightning strikes twice, and you get a 100 percent rate of return for the year again, getting your account back up to $200,000.
- **Year 4:** Ouch! Your funds tank again, you take another 50 percent loss for the year, and your account balance drops back down to $100,000.

Pretty wild ride, huh?

At the start of the fifth year, we get together for one of our periodic reviews. Right out of the gate, you hit me with, "Brian, I am *not* happy. I've given you four years, and I've still got the same amount of money that I started with."

No one could argue against that. It's clear that your actual return over those four years is zero. That doesn't sound like a solid investment. But maybe I'm looking at it in a totally different way? Instead of agreeing with you and seeing what else we could do with your money, I say, "Wait a minute. Let's look at it again. You're doing *great*! Let me show you." Then I grab a pencil and a sheet of paper and say, "You got a 100 percent rate of return the first year, right?" I write 100 at the top of the page. "And then, the second year, you got -50." I write -50 on the next line. "Year three, you got 100 again, and then you got -50 in year four." I write those numbers down the page as well and show him the math as I do it on the paper.

"So, let's see. One hundred *minus* fifty *plus* one hundred *minus* fifty equals . . . one hundred. And one hundred divided by four years leaves us with a 25 percent annual return! Are you telling me you're not happy with a 25 percent annual return on your investment? You should be thanking me!"

This happens daily, and maybe it's misleading. But am I wrong here? That's exactly what happens to most people who don't understand the difference between *average* returns and *actual* returns. In this example, the *average* return was 25 percent, which sure *sounds* good. But the *actual* return—the money the investor actually made—is zero. In this scenario, would you be a happy investor with a 25 percent return that equaled zero dollars? I wouldn't be.

This is the fallacy of chasing investment returns. Refute it all you want, recalculate it a thousand times, do whatever you need to do. Then you'll realize this is *real*, and it happens all the time when investment returns are your guideline in making financial decisions. How many times have you seen or read the disclaimer, "Past performance is not indicative of future results"?

So what do you do? Well, would a Nobel Prize–winning study in economics interest you? In those 401(k) enrollment books, did you ever see a pie chart that looks something like this?

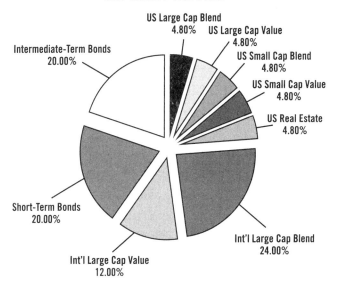

A Diversified Portfolio
60% Stocks / 40% Bonds

This is called *modern portfolio theory*, and Harry Markowitz won the 1990 Nobel Memorial Prize in Economics for this concept. The study said that, of an investor's success in the stock markets:

- 91.5 percent was attributed to how their money was diversified over a broad array of asset classes based on their period and risk tolerance (moderate risk portfolio shown in the chart)
- 4.6 percent was attributed to what investment was chosen (also known as *stock picking* or *chasing returns*)
- 1.8 percent was attributed to market timing (when to buy, when to sell)
- 2.1 percent was attributed to other factors[17]

This study has become the benchmark of the financial advisory world. The risk tolerance questionnaire I mentioned is one of the key components of this method.

Day trading is sexy, and everyone wants to brag about how great they are doing and how they bought Apple at $6 per share. However, based on this study, you can see the minimal success this approach brings over time.

Applying Modern Portfolio Theory

Given the problems I've shown you inherent in chasing returns and picking your own investments, you're probably wondering if there are solutions. Yes, there are. The pie chart on the previous page is uniquely tied to that Nobel Prize–winning study. This is called a *fund of funds* approach.

These *funds of funds* originated for use primarily in the 401(k) world. In seeing the problems I've pointed out and realizing that plan providers (employers) have a fiduciary responsibility to their participants, these *funds of funds* were created to help their participants make the best investment decisions they could, given the lack of advice available to them.

These funds also *manage the fund managers,* meaning if one fund manager isn't performing to the levels set out for their asset class, they can be replaced. Look at the pie chart again. That bottom right section stands for International Large Cap Blend Stocks, which makes up 24 percent of the overall allocation.

If the committee overseeing this moderate risk portfolio determines this particular fund manager is not performing, they have the ability to replace him with another fund manager. This keeps the overall fund running at its optimal level. As an investor in this fund, it's highly unlikely you would ever know this … unless your insomnia drives you to read the fine print on the fund prospectus late at night!

You might know them today as *target-date funds* or *life-style funds,* similar funds that work a little differently based on your specific need. *Lifestyle funds* normally offer five or six investment models to choose from, ranging from conservative to ultra-aggressive. This is where that risk tolerance questionnaire comes into play. For example, say you complete the questionnaire, and it gives you a score. That score identifies a particular model that (ideally) identifies your comfort with risk. If your score equals a moderate risk tolerance, then you allocate 100 percent of your contribution (and the employer's match, if available) into this moderate portfolio.

This pie chart illustrates a "moderate growth" portfolio and shows you how each dollar you contribute is allocated. Remember, 91.5 percent of your success is attributed to how your money is diversified over a broad array of asset classes based on your time frame and personal risk tolerance. It takes the guessing game out of investment selections and helps in matching your money to your emotions.

Target-date funds are similar in their asset allocation approach, except they adjust as you get closer to your targeted retirement date. I'll give you an example, again using nice round numbers. Say it's 2020, and you're forty years old. You plan to retire at seventy, so your *target date* is thirty years from now, meaning that's when you'll need your full retirement income. Since you'll be retiring in 2050, you'd put 100 percent of your allocation into a target date 2050 fund.

What happens to the investments in that fund? They track along with how close you're getting to your target date. As you get older and therefore closer to the target date of 2050, the fund allocation, by design, will reduce the allocation in stock investments and increase the allocation into fixed income investments. The general idea is that your risk tolerance will decrease the closer you get to actually needing that money to replace your income. That is, you don't want to bet your whole nest egg on the latest risky tech start-up six months before you start depending on that retirement account as your sole source of income. This investment strategy closely follows the four phases of your financial life that we unpacked in chapter 8.

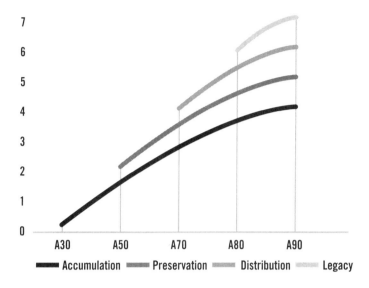

For the majority of my clients who participate in 401(k) plans, and for the sake of simplicity, I really like each of these *funds of funds* strategies. It takes the guesswork out of the equation. However, to be fair and balanced, the internal fund expenses of these types of "fund of funds" may be higher due to the costs of additional management.

I'll close with two observations, one on the lifestyle fund approach, the other on the target-date fund approach. First, if you chose the *moderate risk lifestyle fund*, it will always stay a moderate risk. It never changes. So, it makes sense to occasionally revisit the risk tolerance questionnaire to see if your goals and comfort level still classify as *moderate*. Perhaps as you approach the preretirement stage of your life, you may become more of a *conservative risk* kind of person. In that case, you now know what you'll need to do: make an allocation change so that 100 percent of your account balance and 100 percent of your new contributions will go into the conservative fund. Simple, huh?

Second, with *target-date funds*, you should choose what that targeted date means in your world. Many plan participants assume their date is the date they think they're going to retire, meaning that the fund allocation will be very, very conservative by then.

I tend to disagree with this, primarily based on longevity. A sixty-five-year-old couple has nearly a 50 percent chance of one of them living to age ninety.[18] That means at least one of you will need enough money to live on for twenty-five years (from age sixty-five to age ninety) in retirement. Remember, we want our retirement dollars to outpace inflation and other factors, so being too conservative might work against you while you are now retired.

If you have a family history of long lifespans, then you might consider making your target date *later* than your retirement date. You might argue that you'd be taking too much risk too late in life. I think I'm saying the opposite. Being too conservative too early *is* a big risk in itself, but it's one too many people overlook as they near retirement age. With people living longer than ever, you need to plan your investments such that your distribution phase of life doesn't outpace the money you have in the bank. That puts you in danger of what I consider to be the greatest sin a financial advisor can commit: allowing his client to run out of money!

CHAPTER 22

EMBRACING YOUR INNER NERD: UNDERSTANDING INVESTMENT CONCEPTS, PRODUCTS, AND HOW THEY WORK

I'M CONVINCED THAT ONE OF THE BIGGEST REASONS people don't do more to build wealth and engage with the different wealth-building products on the market is because it's hard to admit they don't understand all the financial lingo associated with investing. How many times have you smiled and nodded along while someone rattled on and on about "the market" or "the S&P" or "the Dow"—even though you had no idea what he or she was talking about? This is bad enough in casual conversation at a dinner party; it's much worse when it's a discussion with your financial advisor. If you really want to build a nice castle, then you need to get your arms around a few basic terms that are too often taken for granted.

What Is a Fiduciary?

First, I want to drill down on a word that I'm hearing a *lot* in advertising of all types, including social media. I'm talking about "the F word": *fiduciary*.

Fiduciary has become somewhat of a buzzword in my world. Per Investopedia, "A fiduciary is a person or organization that acts on behalf of another person or persons, putting their clients' interests ahead of their own, with a duty to preserve good faith and trust."[19] The way I read this means I always put *your* needs and wants ahead of *mine* in all situations, with every product I offer or recommend, 100 percent of the time, with no deviation, period. The way my dad would read it has become my daily mantra: "I never worked a day in my life. I just got up every morning and went out to help people." I can't write this book without putting your needs first. It's not a sales pitch or hidden agenda to sell a product; it's just me continuing to be the professional explainer I've become.

I was talking with my compliance officer about the different ways the word *fiduciary* is used. She said that, since I am registered and affiliated with my broker/dealer, Madison Avenue Securities, that my title is technically an Investment Advisory Representative (IAR) of our firm. Anything and everything I do regarding the recommendation and sale of securities is overseen and reviewed so that my fiduciary responsibilities to you, the client, are being met. In addition, because of my securities licensing, I am a fiduciary in the eyes of the US Securities and Exchange Commission (SEC).

Hopefully, this adds some context the next time you see an advertisement for a financial firm that boldly and proudly declares, "We are fiduciaries." My comment is simple: *so what?* According to the spirit of the term (not the strict legal definition), so am I. If you are in a profession where you put the needs of others ahead of yourself, then you are as well.

With that out of the way, let's dive in. I'll do my best to be as simple as possible, yet as broad as I can as well. There is a plethora of different investment tools available to you today. The ones I want to focus on are probably the most common and widely used, such as:

- Mutual funds
- Exchange Traded Funds (ETFs)
- Individual stocks and bonds
- Turnkey Asset Management Programs (TAMPs)
- Annuities, both fixed and variable

Mutual Funds

The first mutual fund was established in 1924, and it is one of the most common types of investment available today. Mutual funds are usually what's *inside* your company 401(k) or 529 college savings plan, so you probably own mutual funds even if you don't realize it.

A mutual fund is a professionally managed investment portfolio that invests in different types of stocks and bonds, depending on the objectives of the individual fund and fund manager. You purchase these either through an institution such as Fidelity or Vanguard on a "no-load" or no-commission basis, or through a registered representative that might offer a "loaded fund," meaning commissions are paid with each deposit. American Funds, one of the most-used mutual fund families in the country, is one example you may have heard of.

One of the biggest advantages of mutual funds is the ability to own hundreds of different stocks and/or bonds in a single account, which help create diversification and avoid "putting all your eggs in one basket." Because of this, mutual funds also offer a significant level of convenience to the investor.

There are some disadvantages, though. First and foremost, mutual funds have the potential for high internal expenses due to a number of factors, including:

- Buying and selling of the stocks and bonds inside the fund
- Tax inefficiency because of this ongoing internal activity (for nonretirement accounts)
- Poor trade execution

That last one—poor trade execution—can bite you big-time in a couple of ways. First, every time a fund manager buys and sells a stock inside the fund, it creates a taxable event that is passed on to the shareholder, either in the form of a capital gain or ordinary income. Second, the timing of mutual fund transactions can be tricky. Say, for example, your gut and your intuition are telling you that the market is going to crash tomorrow morning, but the market has already closed for the day. You could put a sell order in at the opening bell tomorrow, but that order wouldn't be executed until the *closing* bell later that afternoon. That means you'd still get hit with that day's losses if the market did poorly that day because of the way mutual funds are traded.

Mutual fund managers are governed by the fund *prospectus*—you know, that booklet you get every year and usually throw in the trash or never take out of the envelope it came in. If I am the lead manager for the Carden Small Cap Growth Fund and my prospectus says I can only invest in companies of that size, then that's all I should be investing in—period. Small cap(italization) means a company with $300 million to $2 billion in market size. The prospectus also serves as a full disclosure of the mutual fund's fees and expenses.

So let's say the mutual fund is having a not-so-good year, and I as the fund manager decide we need to bolster returns to hopefully outperform other fund management companies, gain more assets under management, and maybe even get our picture on the cover of *Money* magazine. In order to do so, I buy some of the "FAANG" stocks: Facebook, Amazon, Apple, Netflix, and Alphabet (formerly Google). Am I playing by the rules of our prospectus? Absolutely not! Do you, the fund investor, know this? Highly doubtful! What happens when Small Cap Growth, as an asset class, begins to trend upwards and the FAANG stocks conversely decline? This is called *style drift* and yes, it happens more often than you would think because, as the individual investor putting your faith in this fund manager, all you really care about is the earnings you're receiving. This is one of the biggest disadvantages.

Some of the most popular funds are *index funds*—more specifically, S&P 500 Index funds. Simply put, they invest only in the Standard & Poor's index of 500 of the largest US stocks. They have their pros and cons as well, which I'll talk more about in the next chapter. Also, it is not possible to invest directly in a specific index, but in an index fund.

Exchange Traded Funds (ETFs)

I will disclose another bias: I like exchange-traded funds, or ETFs. They were created in the 1990s as a way to provide access to passive indexed funds to individual investors. In 2020, there were over 7,600 ETFs globally. There's an ETF for whatever you could think of. Want to invest in gold without buying the actual, tangible gold? There's an ETF for that. Want to own an index bigger than the S&P 500? There are multiple types of indexed ETFs.

ETFs trade like stocks and bonds, which solves one of my big problems with mutual funds. Remember, with mutual funds, the trade doesn't settle until the end of day, meaning you can potentially lose money between the opening bell and close of business. But an ETF can be bought and sold on an *immediate basis* (during trading hours). Also, since you're owning an ETF that is tied to a specific index, sector, country, and so on, the underlying investments are rarely traded, making them more tax efficient. ETFs do not charge any commissions like front-end loaded mutual funds, which can legally charge as much as 8.5 percent if disclosed. However, the average loads fall within 3–6 percent, depending on the amount of deposit. If you have an E*trade or other online trading account, the only commissions you pay on the buy and sell of the ETF are what that platform charges, which is generally minimal.

I had an interaction with a friend/client recently that demonstrates both the handiness of ETFs and my fiduciary responsibility as his advisor. A golfing buddy told me he had received a statement from a 401(k) plan through a company he no longer works for. It was around $5,000, and he wanted me to invest it in silver, as he felt silver was the next big thing. I told him that, due to my fiduciary responsibility to him, I would not place that trade. I felt certain it wasn't a prudent choice for him, and I couldn't stand behind that decision. However, I did show him where to find an ETF that invested primarily in silver so he could do the transaction for himself. Several months later, as we were standing on a tee box, I asked, "How's that silver working for you?" He told me that his $5,000 investment was now worth $3,500. Then he asked if he could add it to the portfolio inside his IRA where I had the rest of his money.[20]

Individual Stocks and Bonds

As of this writing, there are more individual online brokerage accounts than ever before. That's because of the ease of buying and selling stocks and bonds. E*trade and TD Ameritrade are the two predominate trading companies that allow individual investors to buy a stock for around $9.99 per trade. Anyone can open a brokerage account to buy, sell, and trade stocks. For many financial professionals, this is all they do for their clients (usually trust accounts and higher net worth individuals).

As a fiduciary, even though stocks might be the best strategy for some consumers, I do not recommend individual stocks to my clients. If they ask, I show them how they can do it for themselves, but I'm an advisor, not a stock picker. I've seen brokerage statements from prospective clients who own a handful of stocks . . . some of which I've never heard of! When I ask why they own them, they say something like, "That's what my guy recommended."

If you know or work with me, you know I'm a walking encyclopedia of sayings, mantras, song lyrics, and so on. Two that come to mind with regard to buying individual stocks are, "Buy what you know," and "Pigs get fat; hogs get slaughtered," meaning greed can come back to bite you in a big way if you're not careful.

Full disclosure: I own individual stocks in one of my personal portfolios, but I know what each company does. Plus, this is where I place some of my discretionary income, meaning I only invest money into single stocks that I can afford to lose. I've already mentioned that the Amazon truck stops often at my home. I watch movies on Netflix. I'm writing this book using Microsoft Word on an Apple computer. I stay in touch with my friends, family, and clients on Facebook. You get the idea. If you come to me with some type of biotech stock, my answer is no. Bitcoin? I studied it quite a bit and honestly still don't know how it works, so I'm not about to invest my *real* coins into it.

In the good old days pre-2008, investment companies would invite advisors to their home offices for workshops and one-on-one dialogues with their fund managers. In one of these gatherings, I found myself in a room full of advisors and a panel of top mutual fund managers when a question came up about Enron. Remember them? One of the biggest scandals of the early 2000s. The managers all agreed that they would never buy the stock because no one could ever figure out what the company actually did. Buy what you know!

Speaking of Enron, I do have one particular framed item on my wall, and that is one share of Enron stock. I have the actual certificate (which you don't see anymore). It's dated March 20, 2003. At its height in 2000, it was trading at almost one hundred dollars per share. One year later, it was basically worthless. Imagine that you were an Enron employee and you had 100 percent of your company 401(k) portfolio in that stock. The company leaders were encouraging you to put all your retirement funds into the stock (which is one of the reasons many went to jail). There was no way you would have sold those shares at its height; now it's worthless, and so is your 401(k) balance. All your retirement funds, gone. Greed overrode logic in this real-world scenario. "Pigs get fat; hogs get slaughtered."

Turnkey Asset Management Programs (TAMPs)

Here's another disclosed bias: I like turnkey asset management programs(TAMPs) for their asset management, diversification, and overall benefits to the client. A TAMP is a fee-based program for asset managers, broker-dealers, and other financial professionals. They can offer technology, back-office support, and tasks such as investment research and asset allocation. Today, there's over $2.75 billion under management in these types of investment portfolios. There are TAMPs that invest in mutual funds, ETFs, and individual stocks . . . or a combination of all of them. Each one has a minimum investment that ranges from $25,000 to as much as $1 million, depending on the needs of the client and the amount of investible assets.

What they enable me to do as an advisor is utilize their expertise so that I can spend more of my time with my clients instead of looking at a computer screen all day trying to buy and sell client accounts and navigate all the ongoing market volatility. It drives me absolutely insane when a prospective client tells me, "My financial advisor manages my money!"—especially when I'm staring at their current statements and see a TAMP I recognize. This tells me the person *thinks* their advisor is personally making great recommendations when I know it's really the TAMP entity that's doing the work.

The way I see it, my job as a financial advisor is to manage *you*, the client, and turn the daily investment decisions over to professionals who manage hundreds of millions, if not billions, of assets. When I say *manage you*, I mean help you navigate all the word garbage of the media, blogs, newsfeeds, and so on. Usually this means it's my job to try to talk you out of cashing everything out when I see you freaking out about the headlines of the day. I like to keep my focus on my clients and trust the super-deep, super-nerdy market analysis to the experts. That's something TAMPs enable me to do.

Of course, there are TAMPs I really like and some I would never, ever use. This is one advantage to being an independent broker: I get to pass on the ones I don't feel are in the best interests of my clients. If you're with an advisor from a national firm, and if that advisor recommends a TAMP with his company's name on it, maybe you should question why. Every hammer needs a nail, right?

Three of the biggest advantages to you, the client, are the portfolio diversification, the liquidity factor, and the fee structure. Unlike mutual funds or annuities, there are no front-end loads nor back-end surrender charges. So if you want to use another advisor and maybe another investment strategy that is more attractive to you for some reason, you can liquidate a TAMP immediately and transfer those assets with no penalties from the surrendering firm. All fees to the investment managers, any trustee fees, and, of course, the advisor fees are fully disclosed on every statement, so you know what you are paying for.

One key disclosure here: I'm only talking about fees inside the actual investment. If the account is an IRA, there could be taxes and penalties (before age fifty-nine and a half) if you withdraw any or all of the account. Also, an individual account (nonretirement), if liquidated, could generate taxable dividends and capital gains.

TAMPs are better known as "fee-based accounts," and I see all-in fees from 1.5 percent to as much as 4 percent, depending on the TAMP internal fees and what the advisor charges. Did you know that an advisor can legally charge as much as a 2.25 percent advisory fee? For comparison, 1 percent is a nice round number for my clients. When I see a brokerage account full of mutual funds with the same family (or a "junk drawer" of a statement where none of the holdings makes any sense whatsoever), and I know a TAMP could be much more efficient for a prospective client, that will be a big part of our conversation without hesitation. If you are working with an advisor, ask them about TAMPs and if they are suitable for you.

One more thing that's worth noting here: I just read a blog post about TAMPs from the FINRA Investor Education Foundation. They said that 63 percent of investors either don't think they pay fees or don't know how much they are paying. To me, that's a serious problem. When talking to an advisor about investing with them, always ask them what the total fee structure looks like. If they say "1 percent," there's a chance they might be talking about their fee only and are not fully disclosing any management fees charged by the underlying investments in the portfolio.

Fixed and Variable Annuities

Once again, here's another of my biases. Depending on the client and their needs, I like properly structured annuity contracts (the operative words being *properly structured*). I've used both variable and fixed annuities for my clients. They can be a part of a well-designed lifetime income plan. All annuities are issued by an insurance company; you're transferring all or a portion of the risk to them. Variable annuities invest in a variety of diversified subaccounts while fixed annuities receive a current yield guaranteed for the contract year with an underlying minimum guaranteed rate throughout the life of the contract.

Most annuity "haters" don't like them because of the higher fee structure and the back-end surrender charges. The fee structure covers the internal expenses and the cost of whatever lifetime benefit riders were built into the contract. Back-end surrender charges occur because, unlike TAMPs, where you pay your fees on an ongoing basis (including advisor compensation), annuities pay the advisor all the compensation up front. Whatever dollar amount was invested into an annuity, the full amount is credited to you and the advisor/agent is paid a commission for the sale of that annuity. The insurance company is at an immediate deficit because of the commissions paid at the point of the sale to the advisor/agent. The surrender charge is structured for a period of years and is based on a declining annual percentage. It reduces each year, so, in the event that you decided to terminate (or surrender) the contract during the surrender period, it recoups the up-front compensation paid to the advisor/agent. I'll talk more about this a little later.

Variable Annuities

Annuities have worked well for my clients by taking all or a portion of the investment risk and all the longevity risk off the table. Variable annuities were a favorite tool for my clients for many years for this and other reasons. In a nutshell, variable annuities are insurance company contracts where the insurance company provides a layer of guarantees for both accumulation and future income. They are sold by prospectus. Most of the contracts I saw utilized the modern portfolio theory method of investing, and the available portfolios in the contracts were primarily risk-adjusted and ranged from conservative to aggressive models. I normally only used these for qualified retirement accounts, like IRA rollovers, when we had little to no liquidity issues before retirement age. For example, if I was working with a fifty-year-old client with $100,000 to invest and we agreed that our time frame for withdrawals was age sixty-five, or fifteen years.

For clients considering variable annuities, I would have explained a variety of possible contract riders and how they could reduce the market risk and longevity risk with that particular account balance. For example, one formerly available rider would have underlying guarantees that, for purposes of future benefits, the account would triple in value over those fifteen years. In addition, we might have added another rider that provided a 5 percent annual withdrawal for life starting at age sixty-five. In this situation, for purposes of a future benefit, my client's annuity would have been worth $300,000 at age sixty-five, and he'd have been able to withdraw $15,000 per year from the account for the remainder of his or her life. Of course, if the investment grew above the guaranteed $300,000, they could have withdrawn 5 percent of whatever that account balance would be. All of this was guaranteed and backed by the particular insurance company providing the variable annuity.[21]

These types of contracts were offered by many major life insurance companies—so many, in fact, there were too many to choose from. But there was a big problem for these variable annuities: just as we saw in the long-term care insurance market, where the insurance companies horribly mispriced the "cost of aging," so the internal fees to maintain these contracts kept going up and up, many all the way up to their maximum allowable amount. That's known as *fee drag,* and it significantly reduced the net returns to the owner. The companies were on the hook to pay these guaranteed benefits, and, one by one, companies either stopped offering these lifetime benefit riders on new contracts (known as GMWB or guaranteed minimum withdrawal benefits), stopped selling those particular variable annuities, or in some cases, got out of the annuity business altogether. However, they could not terminate the contract and the benefits within; they were still responsible to the annuity owner for those lifetime benefits!

For this reason, there's a more limited selection of variable annuities and riders available today, and I don't use them nearly as much as I once did. Although on occasion, they can serve a purpose for a particular client and their financial needs and wants.

Fixed Annuities and Fixed-Index Annuities

Fixed annuities have been around for decades. They pay a stated annual interest rate and a guaranteed rate. A big problem here is that we have been living in a low interest rate environment for a while now. Back in the early eighties when I first started in the business, current yields were anywhere from 8–12 percent. Also, mutual funds and 401(k) plans were in their infancy and the general public didn't have widespread access or awareness of these financial tools, which are now commonplace. Historically, insurance companies primarily used highly rated (also known as "investment grade") bonds to back their fixed annuities and offered an annually stated yield and an underlying guaranteed interest rate inside each contract. Considering the low interest rate environment for bond rates today, many fixed annuities don't hold a lot of attraction these days.

However, there is the advent of the "fixed index annuity," or FIA. Fixed index annuities have the ability to earn interest tied to the performance of an external market index, such as the S&P 500, without ever being invested in the market. These products have limits on what you can earn, so you don't receive all of the index gains and the interest you receive will likely be less than the index. These indexed accounts do not include dividends.

FIAs are conservative financial products and are often used to protect a portion of your principal. When your market index goes down, the worst that can happen is you have zero interest for that year. If the index goes higher on your contract anniversary, you can participate in a portion of the gains through index credits. Most fixed index annuities offer several index and fixed accounts options. You can choose to change indexes or move to fixed accounts as often as once a year.

Where they have become attractive in the last few years, in my opinion, is that in comparison to the rising internal fees of the variable annuity contract, the fee structure is significantly less and oftentimes there are no annual management fees. If you choose the lifetime income benefit rider, that does carry an annual fee.

Annuity Pros and Cons

To wrap up this quick look at annuities, let's break things down into a simple pros / cons list:

Pros

- Longevity risk is transferred to the insurance company.
- Market risk (inside variable annuities) is transferred to the insurance company.
- Great tool to use when building a guaranteed life income strategy, along with Social Security benefits and other client investments.

Cons

- Variable annuities have potentially higher internal expenses than TAMPs or other investments.
- Declining back-end surrender charges (typically seven years or less, declining 1percent per year)
- Lack of liquidity
- Not a good short-term investment. It must be a part of a long-term strategy.
- All commissions are paid to the advisor/agent/sales-person up front, so there's often little accountability going forward for the client. (The compensation ranges on a per-contract basis and is usually between

1–10 percent of the investment amount, per annu-
ities.org.)
- Fixed index annuities only offer a portion of the
  upside potential of the underlying index in exchange
  for insurance company guarantees against loss.

CHAPTER 23

ADVISORS, AGENTS, AND SALESPEOPLE

THERE AREN'T ONLY "GOOD, BAD, AND UGLY" INVEST-ment *products* available to you; there are also "good, bad, and ugly" advisors, salespeople, and agents. I'm sure you've met some of each. For example, one of my social media feeds has been inundated recently with invitations to a free steak dinner as part of a workshop on "tax-free investing." As part of the pitch, they invited me to "read [their] free book on financial freedom." I dug a little further and discovered that they didn't even write *their* free book; they just used another author's work (with permission) to sell their products. That kind of fuzzy advertising drives me crazy and, honestly, gives me a bad impression of the person or firm offering the workshop.

How to Find Out about a Financial Professional

Whenever I get an advertisement for a seminar, workshop, dinner, or webinar, the first thing I do is consult FINRA's BrokerCheck database and see what registrations the person carries.[22] I think you should do the same thing. Unfortunately, there are many wolves in sheep's clothing marketing themselves as comprehensive financial advisors who do not carry *any* of the licensing that I and thousands of advisors do. When I do not see any broker/dealer listings or any other mention of securities-related registrations, it tells me one thing (and it's an important thing for you to know): they are marketing *only* insurance-based products, such as fixed index annuities and universal or whole life policies. Their lack of licensing and registrations severely limits the types of "financial planning" products they're allowed to offer, and they might not meet the requirements necessary to be a fiduciary.

Other Types of Financial Advisors

There are other types of advisors, and I have a lot of peers in the business who have chosen these ways of working with their clients. For example, fee-only planners get paid by charging advisory fees in lieu of commission or fee-based products. Registered Investment Advisors (RIAs) manage assets of individuals and institutional clients. Typically, these advisors get paid via management fees, generally based on a percentage of the assets under management. TAMPs are a popular choice for these advisors because the TAMP itself supplies the research and recommendations. Many of my friends that used to carry insurance licenses and certain securities licenses have gone the route of the RIA, as they work only on a fee basis for advice and assets under management.

You will notice that many advisors have a lot of letters after their name, which means they have passed certain exams. Certified Financial Planner®, or CFP®, is probably the most common. It is obtained through the Certified Financial Planner Board of Standards. There are two designations that are historically more life insurance-based, and they are CLU, or Chartered Life Underwriter, and ChFC, which stands for Chartered Financial Consultant. Both are offered through the American College of Financial Services. There are a plethora of other types of designations out there. If there's a niche market, such as the senior market, or mutual fund specific, there's a designation for it. I've known industry peers who literally had more letters *after* their name than *in* it!

CHAPTER 24

HOW THE MEDIA AFFECTS YOUR EMOTIONS . . . AND YOUR MONEY

*I*MAGINE THIS SCENARIO: YOU'RE IN YOUR CAR AFTER A long day at work, and you turn on talk radio. As you turn up the volume, you hear the announcer say, "The Dow was up fifty points on trading of *blah, blah, blah.*" Some of your retirement savings is invested in the stock market, so you're happy. The market is up; this is good! But what happens the next day when you get in the car and the announcer says the market has dropped today? It's down; are you sad? Of course you are. This information affects you . . . but the effect is primarily emotional.

There's an entire industry built around communicating information about the stock market to the general public, and it's a lucrative one. So it's important we understand the ways that the media—and those controlling the markets—are actually working behind the veil of those radio announcers.

The Dow Jones Industrial Average

In 2004, I wrote a piece called "Dow's Up ... Dow's Down ... Who Cares?" I was doing a lot of workshops and presentations back then, and I always asked the audience, "How many stocks make up the Dow Jones Industrial Average (DJIA)?" The responses were anywhere from the hundreds to the thousands.

The DJIA is a history of the US economy. It was created in 1896 by Charles Dow and Edward Jones to measure the industrial productivity of specific industries in the US, and it's useful in seeing how the economy is doing. But—and here's the shocking thing—the Dow doesn't reflect how *every* company is doing; it only shows us how a handful of stocks are doing. Thirty to be exact...and only thirty! That's because the highly touted Dow Jones Industrial Average is the oldest index in the country, and it has become a benchmark index because of its age. That's it!

If you Google "history of the Dow 30," you'll find some interesting facts. For example, Walmart was placed into the DJIA in 1997. They were a booming example of growth in the retail segment of the index. But for one company to be added, another had to be removed. So guess who Walmart replaced in 1997? Most people think it'd be a company like Kmart, Sears, or JCPenney. Wrong, wrong, and wrong. They replaced Woolworth. If you're a millennial or Gen Xer, go ask your parents about Woolworth. Today, they are pretty much nonexistent.

If I take a slowly dying company like Woolworth *out* of the index and place a high-growth company like Walmart *into* the index, what do you think will happen? The Dow will suddenly shoot up, seemingly out of nowhere. Everyone will get excited, thinking that the whole market is on the rise, but in reality, all that happened was that an underperforming stock was replaced by a high-performing stock on the DJIA. As a result, general consumer confidence goes up, and the economy gets better for a little while.

Here's why a general understanding of the DJIA matters: if you know how the game is played, you can start to understand what's going on behind the scenes when you hear alarming news reports about the economy. For example, I'm sure you remember 2008, when markets fell 40 percent one week in September. Wall Street totally mucked up Main Street, and American International Group (AIG) became one of the companies deemed "too big to fail." They were guaranteeing all the mortgage-backed securities issued by Merrill Lynch, Bear Stearns, and Goldman Sachs. As a result of their gross mismanagement and loss of value, AIG was removed from the DJIA. Guess who replaced them?

Hmm, let's see . . . a global insurance and pension company goes down hard. Who to put in their place? *How about Kraft Foods?* The stock market plummets in 2008 and everyone knows what Americans do in times of financial crisis: *we eat.* Cheez Whiz and Velveeta for everyone! Soon, the stock market soared in a "Great Recovery." A few years later, when the media was laser-focused on the passing of Obamacare, Kraft Foods left the index, only to be replaced by…UnitedHealth Group, a health care company!

The decisions being made about which thirty companies make it into the DJIA and at what time are important, because they directly impact our emotions about the economy in general and our personal financial health in particular. The reality is that a rise in the Dow *might* be the result of an economic boom . . . or it might be the result of a handful of decision-makers moving the pieces around on the board to make things look better. Either way, I don't want to let other people dictate how I feel about my money.

The S&P 500

The Standard & Poor's 500 Index (S&P) is similar to the DJIA, but it is much more comprehensive. The S&P was introduced in 1923 when it started tracking a small number of stocks—primarily to compete with the DJIA. In 1926, however, it grew to ninety stocks; it expanded to five hundred stocks in 1957.

The operative word in Standard & Poor's 500 Index is *index*. It's just a benchmark and comparison tool. The problem is that you, the individual investor, probably think all five hundred stocks are equally weighted inside the index. It's a common thought. However, here's how it plays out.

As of January 2021, the total market capitalization of the companies in the index was $31.61 trillion. The largest member was Microsoft at $1.64 trillion, making up 5.78 percent of the total S&P index. The smallest was H&R Block at $2.8 billion, which makes up only .01 percent of the index. Given the outsized power Microsoft holds over the S&P, what do you think would happen if their stock experienced a 10 percent increase in a single day? Easy: the entire S&P would rise.

On the other end of the spectrum, what would happen if H&R Block reported record-shattering numbers during next year's tax season financial quarter? I'm sure H&R Block's value would rise, but it wouldn't put a dent in the overall S&P. In fact, H&R Block could go up 1,000 percent in a single day, and it wouldn't cause much more than a ripple in the S&P.[23]

Nasdaq

The other number that is reported daily is the Nasdaq, which is another stock exchange that was created by the National Association of Securities Dealers (NASD) to enable investors to trade securities on a computerized, fast, and transparent system. The term *Nasdaq* refers to an index called the Nasdaq Composite, which includes over three thousand stocks. You will see most of the "big tech" stocks listed here. Once again, it's an index; it's just newer than the S&P 500 and the Dow Jones indexes.

Financial Fiction

One of my nationally known mentors that I regularly read calls investment-based magazines *financial pornography*. That's a pretty strong term, so I'll just call it *financial fiction*. After many years of watching the ebb and flow of the bulls and the bears in this business, I've seen my share of misinformation. However, my professional experience, education, and beliefs as a financial advisor allow me to know the difference between financial fiction and reality.

I like old westerns. They're always a surprising place to find wit and witticisms that are as true in our time as they were in the age of cowboys. The movie *The Man Who Shot Liberty Valance,* starring Jimmy Stewart, is particularly relevant to those of us who have developed a growing distrust of the obvious biases of the news industry. In the film, the hero is neither made nor born, but *manufactured* by the so-called journalists of the time. As the newspaper editor in the film said, "This is the West. When the legend becomes the fact, print the legend."[24]

I believe today's financial news is printing the legend. Below are just a few examples of financial fiction I've seen in popular financial magazines lately. Let's address these Liberty Valance–style, separating the legend from the facts.

> **LEGEND:** You don't need a financial advisor to create wealth. Just do it yourself!
>
> **FACT:** From its inception in 1926 to year ending 2019, the S&P 500 average annual return was 9.96 percent, but the average investor only made 5.04 percent.[25] Emotion plays so much into prudent investor behavior. This annual return assumes a "buy and hold" strategy throughout, with no withdrawals or liquidating to cash in a down market. It's the advisor's role to guide you through the volatility of the markets and to keep you on track to meet your financial goals.

LEGEND: Knowing what stocks to buy and sell and how to time the market is the key to wealth accumulation in investments.

FACT: A Nobel Prize–winning study found that marketing timing was only responsible for 2 percent and investment selection was only responsible for 4 percent of investing success. The remaining 94 percent of success was attributed to *asset allocation* via modern portfolio theory.[26]

LEGEND: We each have plenty of time to save for retirement.

FACT: Per ValuePenguin, the median bank account balance in 2019 was only $5,300 per household in America.[27] The average total savings for Americans in their 50s was $117,000.[28]

LEGEND: The Dow Jones Industrial Average and the S&P 500 Index are the leading indicators of how the US stock market is faring.

FACT: Only thirty stocks make up the entire DJIA, and 22 percent of the largest companies in America are not part of the S&P index (source: Russell, Inc.).

So the next time you find yourself taking some bit of financial "wisdom" for granted, ask yourself, "Where did I get this information? Have I ever actually researched this, or do I just assume what I've heard is correct? Do I know this for a fact, or could it be a legend?"

Be aware of how this daily information affects you and whether it really matters to you at all. If you're in a truly diversified portfolio where only a moderate percentage is in US large cap growth and income stocks (which is where the S&P 500 Index falls), then only a small percentage of your overall portfolio is even participating in these daily reports. Hopefully, this little history lesson changed your perspective and settled your emotions a bit.

CHAPTER 25

THE FOUR QUADRANTS OF INVESTOR BEHAVIOR

*I*N 2002, PSYCHOLOGIST DANIEL KAHNEMAN WON THE Nobel Memorial Prize in Economic Sciences. Wait, how does a psychologist get an award in economics? His work was groundbreaking at the time, and today it's a widely discussed subject in the investing world. In a nutshell, Kahneman's "behavioral economics" studied how psychological, emotional, cultural, and social factors affected the decisions of individuals and institutions and how those decisions varied from traditional economic theory. Basically, he looked at how emotions override intellect when it comes to investing.

Kahneman also got into "hedonic psychology," which is the study of what makes one's life experiences pleasant or unpleasant. Does happiness come from what you experience here and now? Or perhaps it's connected to some form of "life satisfaction" from achieving goals and meeting expectations?

This is heady material I file under "stuff that makes me fun at parties."

Look at the graph below.

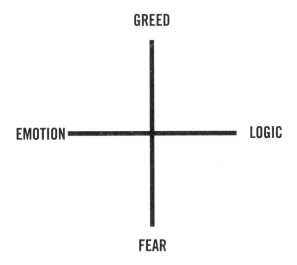

I came up with this graph two decades ago, and I've been writing it on napkins for people ever since. It helps me find out what a person's actual tolerance for risk might be. In my role as a "professional explainer," this helps get my point across and maybe differentiate myself from the other financial advisors out there.

You see that Fear and Greed are polar opposites on the vertical line, and Emotion and Logic are opposite on the horizontal line. These four factors create quadrants.

First, let's consider the Emotion/Logic horizontal line. Logically, you know you should be putting money away into some form of investment accounts, whether it's your 401(k) plan, your IRA, an individual portfolio of stocks and bonds, and/or maybe even investment real estate. But emotionally, you might be overcome with a need to hide all your money under your mattress, stick it in a "safe" money market account, or even blow it all on a massive spending spree to medicate yourself after a bad day at work. When emotion and logic butt heads, emotion usually wins.

Next, look at the Greed/Fear vertical line. Imagine your investment accounts soaring in value. It would feel great, right? Why? Because of greed. However, once the market corrects and you see double-digit losses in that same portfolio, the fear of losing money takes over and you pull all your money out of what was supposed to be a long-term investment. The problem is, you cashed out at the worst possible time—at the bottom of a 15 or 20 percent drop. You might think you're winning by stemming your losses, but you actually lost by getting out of the game. If you had stayed fully invested, those losses would have remained strictly "paper losses." Once you made the decision to bail, however, those losses became *real*.

Albert Einstein said it best: "No problem can be solved from the same level of consciousness that created it." This basically means when you're emotional, it's hard to solve your own problems or dilemmas.

For example, picture a widow living on Social Security who invested in very low-yielding CDs. Where does she fall on this quadrant? Well, she's obviously full of the fear of losing money and is quite emotional about it. Inflation risk is slowly eating away at her purchasing power, but her emotional state will not let her do anything to improve her situation.

Conversely, someone who is using an investment port-folio that is based on their time frame and risk tolerance would be one that I would say is using logic in their thinking. If you've ever answered a risk tolerance questionnaire, you might have been asked, "How would you react if the value of your long-term investments declined by 20 percent in one year?" If you said you would be "very concerned," then emotion and fear might be driving the correct investment strategy for you, which could be a more conservative strategy. If you said, "I'm a long-term investor and wouldn't freak out about a 20 percent decline," that shows a more logical mindset and potentially you would be comfortable investing into a more growth-oriented, if not aggressive, strategy.

From 1926 to 2019, the S&P 500 Index average return was almost 10 percent, but the average investor made *half* that. Can you guess why that is? Their investment strategies were incorrectly matched to their emotions, and when the market got tough, they went to the sidelines and got out!

Are there solutions? Yes, of course there are. Your company 401(k) plan should provide a risk tolerance ques-tionnaire. Find it, complete it, and see how you fare. If you were my client and I was looking to share an asset allocation strategy, I would ask you to complete the same type of ques-tionnaire so we could determine what mix of equities and fixed income would meet our chosen objectives while honing in on your emotional comfort level in managing the constant volatility of the investment markets.

Periodically retaking your risk tolerance assessment, either online through your 401(k) or with your advisor, is always a prudent decision. The markets will always be volatile, but it's those who can manage the rough times who will generally win in the end.

CHAPTER 26

SOCIAL SECURITY AND HOW IT FACTORS INTO YOUR LIFETIME INCOME PLANNING

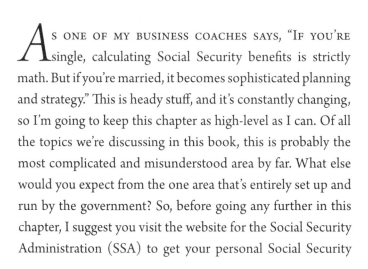

A S ONE OF MY BUSINESS COACHES SAYS, "IF YOU'RE single, calculating Social Security benefits is strictly math. But if you're married, it becomes sophisticated planning and strategy." This is heady stuff, and it's constantly changing, so I'm going to keep this chapter as high-level as I can. Of all the topics we're discussing in this book, this is probably the most complicated and misunderstood area by far. What else would you expect from the one area that's entirely set up and run by the government? So, before going any further in this chapter, I suggest you visit the website for the Social Security Administration (SSA) to get your personal Social Security benefit statement.[29] That way, you can track this chapter more easily.

Social Security was not designed to be the *only* retirement income plan for eligible US citizens. At best, it was a supplemental plan primarily meant to create a federal safety net for elderly, unemployed, and disadvantaged Americans. However, Social Security has now become a cornerstone of most people's retirement planning, and that's brought a whole new level of complexity no one ever intended.

Social Security as we know it dates back to 1935 when the Social Security Act was signed into law by President Franklin Roosevelt. The first Social Security benefits were paid in 1937, and those early checks were one-time payments. In 1939, the program was expanded to include dependents and survivors of workers who retire, are disabled, or die prematurely. The first monthly check went out in 1940, and they've been mailing them out by the bushel every month since then.

Now, think back to what life was like in those days. Life expectancy at birth in 1930 was indeed only fifty-eight for men and sixty-two for women, and the retirement age was sixty-five. Social Security benefits were simply not designed to extend decades into retirement, covering modern lifespans into our eighties, nineties, and beyond. Plus, back then, the typical worker stayed at the same company or factory their entire working years and was probably eligible for a monthly lifetime pension and lifetime health care. There was no real savings plan like today's 401(k).

For people born in or after 1960, the personalized benefit statement on the SSA website only tells you how much you are eligible for at ages sixty-two (only 66 ⅔ percent of what you could collect if you waited until age sixty-seven), sixty-seven (what they consider your full retirement age [FRA], when you're eligible for "full" Social Security benefits), or age seventy. What it doesn't tell you is that you can actually "phase out" your SS benefits by continuing to generate an earned income.

Let's say I'm sixty-two, and because it's what everyone else is doing, I go ahead and start taking the $1,800/month benefits I qualify for. But I'm still working, and I make around $53,000/year. I have made two significant errors.

First, I've locked in my monthly benefit for the remainder of my life, which is only 66 2/3 percent of the benefit I would have collected if I'd waited until my FRA to start collecting.

In addition, I've double-crossed myself because I have elected a monthly benefit payment that I might not receive because my earned income from my job exceeds the limit for receiving benefits at age sixty-two, not including income from retirement plans, real estate, or investments.

"Okay," I might say, "I've decided to wait until I reach my full retirement age as far as Social Security is concerned, but it's not taxable, right?" Wrong. Depending upon your provisional income (gross income not including Social Security + tax-free interest, such as from a municipal bond + 50 percent of your Social Security benefit) and filing status (single/married), up to 85 percent of your benefit could be added back to your income for taxation purposes. As of 2021, the provisional income limit is $34,000 if you are single and $44,000 if you are married filing jointly (limits are subject to change annually). I highly suggest seeking professional advice when determining your tax liability, as obviously this can be complicated and very tricky.

So, if I'm single with no spouse, my decision on when and how to elect my benefits is pretty simple. When I turn sixty-seven, I can begin to receive 100 percent of my full Social Security monthly benefits for the remainder of my life. When I die, it stops.

However, if I'm married, it takes strategy and planning. The underlying point is that deciding when to take Social Security is not a cut-and-dried issue. In my office, we use a tool called a Social Security optimizer to show our clients the best time to elect receipt of their benefits. Between your full retirement age of sixty-seven and age seventy, your benefit increases 8 percent per year. So if you elect to receive your Social Security benefits at age sixty-seven, you would receive 100 percent of your eligible benefits. However, by waiting three years until age seventy to start collecting benefits, your monthly benefit will have grown to 124 percent.

Let's look at my hypothetical life again, in which I'm married. We'll assume my wife will have a longer life expectancy than me, so I will defer taking benefits until age seventy. As stated, every year from my FRA of age sixty-seven to age seventy, my benefits grow or "step up" by 8 percent annually. At age seventy, then, I will receive 124 percent of my full Social Security benefits. Assuming my benefits exceed those of my spouse, and assuming she survives me when I die, she will stop receiving her personal benefit, assume *my* 124 percent benefit amount, and continue receiving it until her death.

This is key because, as an advisor, there is nothing I can offer that provides a guaranteed 8 percent step-up for three years. Again, as I said earlier, this benefit is significant and, more importantly, *guaranteed* by the Social Security Administration.

If you choose to go to the Social Security office and attempt to meet with an employee who is designated to help you, guess what? They are not allowed to give any advice to you whatsoever. None. Zip. Nada. So, what do you do? The question you should be asking yourself right now, assuming you're in that window of age fifty-five to sixty-five is, "Does my advisor have the correct tools to help me and my spouse optimize our Social Security?" If not, it's time to be asking around! Social Security benefit planning is a big part of retirement income planning, which we will discuss very soon in a future chapter.

CHAPTER 27

THE DIFFERENT TYPES OF RISKS AND HOW THEY AFFECT YOU

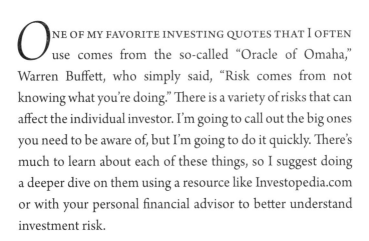

ONE OF MY FAVORITE INVESTING QUOTES THAT I OFTEN use comes from the so-called "Oracle of Omaha," Warren Buffett, who simply said, "Risk comes from not knowing what you're doing." There is a variety of risks that can affect the individual investor. I'm going to call out the big ones you need to be aware of, but I'm going to do it quickly. There's much to learn about each of these things, so I suggest doing a deeper dive on them using a resource like Investopedia.com or with your personal financial advisor to better understand investment risk.

Market Risk

There are three main types of market risk to be aware of.

Equity risk refers to the volatility of stock investing, which means the stock price fluctuates in the market. In today's world, those fluctuations occur minute by minute.

Interest rate risk is mostly felt in bonds as interest rates are strongly tied to the bond market. When interest rates rise, the price and value of a bond falls. Conversely, when interest rates fall, the bond prices and values rise.

Currency risk applies to those who invest in foreign markets. If you've traveled outside the US and have seen the exchange rates for the American dollar versus that country's dollar, you have experienced currency risk.

Liquidity Risk

This is the risk of not being able to sell your investments when you wish. This means you might have to sell it at a loss for the liquidity you require. "Buy low, sell high," right? Remember earlier when I talked about having margin? This is why. You may not be *able* to sell high when you need to sell. A perfect example is your 401(k) account during your working years, especially prior to age fifty-nine-and-a-half.

Concentration Risk

Concentrating too much of your money in a single invest-ment puts everything at risk. I'm sure you've heard the saying, "Don't put all your eggs in one basket." This is what it's referring to, and it's a good argument for diversifying your portfolio.

Credit Risk

This focuses primarily on the bond market. If a company is struggling to meet its obligations, the rating agencies such as Standard & Poor's or Moody's could change their ratings and the investment could devalue.

Insurance companies and banks typically invest in *investment grade* bonds, which are rated BB to AA+. These are used to back savings accounts, CDs, annuity rates, and, of course, cash values in permanent contracts. The other type you know as *junk bonds*, meaning they are rated less than BB and therefore carry more risk to the investor.

Reinvestment Risk

This is when you may have a specific investment, say an older CD that was paying you 5–6 percent, that reaches maturity. You want to reinvest that money, but the options you have now offer significantly lower returns, say 2–3 percent. This is more common than you realize for people who are ultra–risk averse. Back when interest rates were much higher than they are today, your grandparents could live quite comfortably on their CD interest. Sadly, those days appear to be gone . . . at least for the foreseeable future.

Inflation Risk

Inflation is like the wind: you can't *see* it, but you can *feel* it. Look at the cost of virtually everything compared to where prices were ten years ago. As I sit here writing this, the cost of building materials and lumber for new housing has increased over 60 percent in the last year. Ask your parents what their first house cost, and then go price a comparable one for yourself. That's inflation!

Your spending power can be greatly affected down the road in your later years if you don't invest prudently and wisely now. If you're getting a 1 percent savings rate and inflation is averaging 3 percent, you may think you're winning the game, but you are actually losing big-time! Your savings aren't growing fast enough to keep up with inflation, meaning the *buying power* of those dollars is shrinking, even though the cash balance is growing (slowly).

Horizon Risk

Horizon risk is anything that shortens your investment horizon. For example, I've had many clients who were working toward a retirement age of sixty-five, only to be caught in a company downsizing/offshoring/elimination of employees in their late fifties or early sixties. They were counting on the growth inside their company 401(k) plan along with the company match and benefits! Because of their horizon shortening, we had to totally rebuild their retirement income plans.

Longevity Risk

This is the risk of outliving your money, and it's the greatest challenge facing many people today. As an advisor, it's my job to help you do all you can to avoid this outcome. Social Security is something you cannot outlive, but it's not the end all, be all. In a perfect world, we'd take the lowest risk possible while getting the highest return. Yeah, right. Don't we all wish that were possible! This is the basis of modern portfolio theory and diversification. Fundamentally, the only way to get a higher return is to take higher, more calculated risk.

It's scary when you put all these risks together, isn't it? To me, the "big three" are market risk, inflation risk, and longevity risk. This is where the *financial psychologist* and *professional explainer* in me really come to life. With all these different risks in mind, which ones do you fear the most? What are you doing today to guard yourself against these risks?

CHAPTER 28

PLANNING FOR YOUR INCOME IN RETIREMENT

———✦———

H OPEFULLY, YOU RECOGNIZE THE IMAGE BELOW. THIS
is the highest peak on the planet, Mount Everest. I
was in an advisor workshop a few years back, and the speaker
posed this question: "When do you think people die on
Mount Everest? Going up . . . or coming down?" It resonated
with me so much that I find myself asking this question a lot
in client meetings.

Understandably, most people think the biggest dangers occur when you're going up. That seems to be the most difficult part, right? My clients are shocked when I tell them more people die coming down Mount Everest. But think about it: You've gotten to the mountaintop. The adrenaline rush is off the charts! You've accomplished a major lifetime goal. You made it! But now, you're tired, exhausted, and oxygen-deprived, and you're in a bigger rush to get *down* than you were to get to the *top*. That's where the accidents and missteps happen most often. Make sense?

Once they get the point I'm making about Everest, I shift the discussion back to their retirement. I ask, "When do you think people fail in retirement: during the Accumulation (ascent) phase or the Distribution (descent) phase?" They get my point.

Traditional financial planning says that if you save and invest X number of dollars over Y number of years at an average annual return of (fill in the blank), you will have Z dollars at a specific age. In addition, if you structure your withdrawals at a specific annual percentage of your total retirement account balance and live to your life expectancy—with zero life events along the way—congratulations! You've got a successful retirement plan.

Years ago, I was invited to speak to an investment club of retired engineers. Most of them were DIY guys. They knew everything. They saw the cost of a fee-based planner that either charged an advisory fee, an hourly fee, or a commission as a total waste of money and dollars that they could have invested to earn a higher return.

I asked this group, "In retirement, which would you rather have: a big pile of money or an income that you could not outlive?" Guess what their answer was? Yep, they wanted a big pile of money! I want to pose that question to you right now. Which would you prefer?

As we start thinking about income in retirement, most planners see it as a game of checkers. You make this move. Then you make that move. You see what the board gives you, you make a couple more moves, and maybe you win the game.

I don't see it that way. Your personal financial plan should be seen as a game of financial chess. You should be planning a specific series of moves that are surrounded by a unique set of strategies. Each move on the board is designed to set up future moves later in the game so that you can win the game with a greater chance of certainty.

In retirement income planning, if we've built your plan correctly, we should be looking at a predictable outcome, and we should have either minimized or mitigated the things that could have or did go wrong. You may think your retirement income will come solely from "a big pile of money" in your IRA or 401(k) withdrawals, but that's much less likely than you think. In reality, your income stream will flow from a few different places, each representing a different financial strategy. In total, these different "buckets of money" create an income that will stick with you throughout your retirement lifetime. It's that stable source of cash flow, not a pile of money, that makes the difference. And that is the result of a variety of strategies, just like chess.

One of the biggest dilemmas in retirement planning today is the focus on *wealth accumulation*. Dr. Robert Merton wrote an article in *Harvard Business Review* in July 2014 titled "The Crisis in Retirement Planning." What is this *crisis*? Merton explains, "Our approach to saving is all wrong: We need to think about monthly income, not net worth."[30] If you follow the beliefs of traditional planning, you will immediately cut yourself off from several key pieces of the plan we're building for long-term income in retirement.

Would it make sense to take a portion of your retirement account (I didn't say all!) and purchase some type of annuity that will provide guaranteed income for the rest of your life and the life of your spouse? Would it make sense to seek the advice of a competent advisor that understands how to use these financial tools to optimize your retirement dollars and maybe avoid the minefield of problems that might lie ahead?

Sources of Retirement Income

Traditional financial planning basically says that prudent saving and investment strategies throughout your life should enable you to:

- Have a reasonable rate of long-term growth that provides enough monthly income to meet or exceed your needs in your later years.
- Afford the life events I've talked about throughout this book, such as the need for long-term care for either you, your spouse, or perhaps your aging parents or special-needs children.

- Have enough left over after you're gone that your
  heirs, such as adult children and their children, will
  have some form of inheritance.

Remember the question I asked that investing group about whether they wanted a big pile of money or an income they couldn't outlive? Those who preferred the pile of money had bought into that traditional investment thought process.

I work with a lot of unique clients from all occupations, industries, and backgrounds. In creating retirement income strategies, my primary objective is to get them to expand their thinking away from that traditional way of thinking. Some advisors use the "bucket approach," while others use spreadsheets. But I am old school, so I'm usually in front of a whiteboard during our strategy sessions.

I start by drawing a circle in the middle of the board, which I label "Total Retirement Income." This is home base. This represents every dollar the person will have coming in each month during retirement. Then I draw circles all around the Total Retirement Income bubble. These are the potential sources of income that will feed into the center circle. In this example, we'll have nine. Many of these income sources fit into the traditional thought process, but I really want to broaden their perspective, so I include things most people have never considered. Seeing it drawn out visually right in front of them helps enormously. Maybe it'll help you too.

Sources of Income While in Retirement

Let's go through each one, working counterclockwise.

Rollover IRA from former company retirement plans, 401(k), and maybe a SEP-IRA. We need a growth-oriented strategy here to offset inflation and longevity risks. Turnkey Asset Management Programs (TAMPs) are usually my go-to because there are no up-front commissions or back-end surrender charges, and we can make a change with no adverse consequences to the client.

Annuities. Here is where a properly positioned annuity can be a great tool, as it can give a guaranteed lifetime monthly income with no downside risk. It also serves as the fixed income portion of our asset allocation strategy. We basically can create a "pension-like" cash flow, and it should have a long-term time frame.

Social Security benefits. Remember, if you are single, it's math; if you're married, it's planning. Social Security should be considered as another guaranteed lifetime monthly income strategy.

Individual brokerage accounts, such as E*trade, and so on. This is where your individual stock portfolio sits, and the challenge here is how to create liquidity for periodic withdrawals. ETFs work well here also.

Home Equity Lines of Credit (HELOCs) are good tools to have in retirement—not so much for income purposes, but for emergencies such as health-care expenses or household purchases/repairs. This strategy helps keep you as fully invested as possible by not having to liquidate assets at the wrong time. Again, a HELOC is one of your cash or cash equivalents.

Investment real estate, once debt-free, acts like a monthly pension check if managed correctly. It also offers tax advantages to offset taxation of other investments. Real estate offers growth through appreciation, income through rents, tax advantages through depreciation, and so on. This is a great asset to own, but be sure to use a real estate professional who truly knows this market.

Permanent life insurance, which should have been purchased at least 5–10 years before retirement. This gives you:

- Tax-free use of accumulated cash values via loans and withdrawals
- Tax-free withdrawals for long-term care needs by utilizing the riders built into the policy

- Tax-free death benefits that will replenish the investment plans from which you have been deriving
  monthly income
- A legacy of love via inheritances to your children,
  grandchildren, charities, and so on, all of which are
  100 percent income tax–free to the beneficiaries

1099 Income, just because you still feel the need to
work and give back. What's the quote from *The Shawshank
Redemption*? "Get busy living or get busy dying."[31] My dad
worked a few days a week up until he was eighty-four, when
his health declined. He just loved being in the mix.

Roth IRA and Roth 401(k) accounts. Now you get to
enjoy the feeling of tax-free withdrawals as you have already
paid taxes on the "seed" and the harvest is all yours.

As you can see, there are a myriad of strategies from
which to derive and optimize your income in retirement, all
the while working through the minefield of risks discussed in
chapter 27. This is where a prudent and duly licensed financial
advisor can become a great asset. By having most, if not all, of
these tools available, they can create some unique and tailor-
made strategies so you can enjoy those "golden years" and live
with financial certainty.

CHAPTER 29

ALTERNATIVE INVESTMENT STRATEGIES, AKA NONQUALIFIED PLANS

*E*VEN THOUGH THEY COME IN DIFFERENT SHAPES AND sizes and are known by different names, numbers, and initials, there are really only two types of investment accounts in America: *qualified plans* and *nonqualified plans*. Most people who are actively investing are participating in some kind of qualified plan. *Qualified* means it has a special tax treatment in the eyes of the Internal Revenue Service. IRAs, Simplified Employer Pension (SEP) plans, 401(k) plans, 403(b) plans, profit sharing, and pension plans are the most common. All these plans are governed by the Employee Retirement Income Security Act (ERISA).

Since they are *qualified* in the eyes of the IRS and the US government, guess who makes up the rules? Exactly . . . *they* do. I've talked about some of the pitfalls of managing (and mismanaging) money in these kinds of accounts in earlier chapters. Now I want to turn our attention to *nonqualified plans* for a few minutes.

What is a nonqualified plan? Well, it's exactly what the name implies. It's not qualified in the eyes of the IRS and the government for tax purposes, and it falls outside ERISA guidelines. The bad news is that this means these investments aren't tax deductible like the aforementioned qualified plans are. The good news, though, is that this also means the government doesn't get to make the rules for when you put money in and, more importantly, how you take money out.

Companies may dabble in nonqualified plans, usually as a way to provide additional benefits for key executives. What's much more common, though, are individuals who invest in non-market-based securities, like real estate. The people who come into my office with real wealth usually built it not through a qualified plan like a 401(k) but through a nonqualified option like real estate or business ownership.

The old "defined benefit pension plan" that gave our parents and grandparents the promise of a monthly check that neither spouse could outlive is gone! Today, the onus is on us to fund our own retirements . . . and we as a society are failing badly.

Remember, I'm about as comprehensive in my practice as anyone you will ever meet. In fact, many of my clients own rental real estate in lieu of funding retirement accounts. Why is this a good idea for some? If you think of all the different investments available to you, they have three distinct characteristics:

1. Growth
2. Income
3. Tax Advantages

An individual stock will give you growth via share price increase and income via dividends, but it provides no tax advantages. An individual bond will give you income via interest payments and, depending on the type of bond, might pay interest that is tax-free, but you get little to no growth. But what about investment real estate? How does that withstand the growth/income/tax stress test?

Let's say I purchased a duplex as an investment property in 2005. At the time, I asked three questions:

1. *Will it offer growth through appreciation?* Yes, it's very possible.
2. *Will it pay me an income through rents?* If properly managed, yes, of course it will.
3. *Does it offer any tax advantages?* Yes, rental real estate offers several tax benefits, such as depreciation and deductions on mortgage interest, insurance, maintenance, and property taxes.

I've never seen another investment that checks all three boxes![32]

What might my long-term play have been with this duplex? If I were going back in time to 2005 and making this purchase, I'd probably adopt an "income later" strategy. That is, my immediate goal would be using the monthly rental income to pay off the mortgage balance as quickly as possible.

Once the rent has paid off the mortgage after fifteen years or so, I'd be left with a debt-free property, with each side of the duplex earning about $2,000 a month in rents in my current market. At that point, I would have created a monthly income for myself that, if managed properly, would last me my lifetime and could be passed on to my family after I'm gone, thereby giving them not just a *house*, but a *performing asset* that's generating monthly income.

Now, is the income taxable? Of course it is! But it's hitting my mailbox every month regardless of market conditions, political changes, and all the other stresses that affect my retirement income strategies, such as my 401(k) and IRA distributions.

If this appeals to you, there are two key people you need to have at your conference table: a good Realtor and a mortgage lender. They are the ones who will create the entrance strategies and find the appropriate property for you. I can crunch numbers with the best of them, but it's these two professionals that you need to engage.

CHAPTER 30

LIVING A LIFE OF SIGNIFICANCE AND LEAVING A LEGACY OF LOVE

*I*N CHAPTER 8, WHERE WE TALKED ABOUT THE IMPORTANT matter of life insurance, I introduced you to the four phases of your financial life using the following chart:

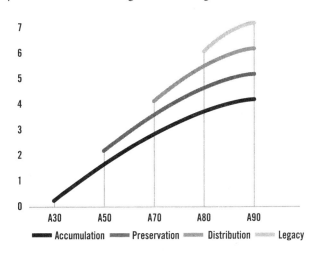

Remember how this works? You go through four financial phases as you get older. You start with Accumulation, then move into Preservation, then begin Distribution, and finally move into Legacy.

Once you hit Distribution mode, you have worked your financial plan well. You've avoided multiple events where life could have gone very differently, and now you're planning for retirement. The kids are grown and gone, there are grandchildren in the picture—maybe even great-grandchildren! And you, of course, having a heart and soul, want to leave a legacy of love for your family or perhaps charities that you have a passion for. So, how do you do it?

Many financial planners focus strictly on Accumulation and Distribution and completely ignore Preservation and Legacy. This is where traditional planning fails in my mind. People who don't use a financial advisor wind up in this situation all too frequently—and many who *do* use a financial advisor find their advisor does not believe in this strategy...but I do!

Picture this: You and your spouse are both sixty-five years old, and you've funded a nice retirement account worth $1 million. You've had a health scare or two, but you're a survivor. Now, it's time to face another type of risk that far too many financial advisors neglect: longevity risk, or the risk of outliving your savings.

According to a recent *Wall Street Journal* article:

- A sixty-five-year-old man has a 41 percent chance of living to age eighty-five and a 6 percent chance of living to age ninety.

- A sixty-five-year-old woman has a 53 percent chance of living to age eighty-five and a 13 percent chance of living to age ninety.
- If the man and woman are married, the chance that at least one of them will live to any given age is increased. There's a 72 percent chance that one of them will live to age eighty-five. There's even an 18 percent chance that one of them will live to age ninety-five![33]

Yes, you read that right, and it's from a legitimate source!

So, you've accumulated $1 million in retirement savings. Your home is paid for, the kids are grown, and now you're both ready to enjoy the golden years. How are you feeling about that $1 million nest egg at this point? Did I get you thinking a bit here? Good. John Lennon said it best: "Life is what happens to you while you're busy making other plans."[34]

Let's add a new wrinkle. That inexpensive term life policy you bought online thirty years ago has expired, there's no way to convert it to a new ongoing policy past its level premium period, and there's no way you can get another term life policy at that price. You also passed on the long-term care plan your advisor recommended many years ago, thinking it was too expensive. You preferred to keep your sights set on maximizing that retirement account, which has now technically made you a millionaire. All your eggs are in that one basket. That's where your entire retirement income will come from for however long you both live. Good thing that one domino is still standing!

But what's endangering that $1 million lifeline? Go back and review the list of risks in chapter 27. What other risks will you face for the next twenty or thirty years? I could fill in fifteen to twenty different life events here, but I think I've already covered a lot of them so far.

What's your strategy now? You've accumulated and preserved. Now you're in Distribution mode, and you want to live a comfortable retirement without running out of money, *and* you want to leave a legacy of love to your heirs.

Now's the time to stop reading, back away from the book, and visualize what that is going to look like. (This statement is designed to make you uncomfortable, by the way.)

You have one plan and one plan only. You must get conservative with your investing and use an interest-only strategy for retirement income, meaning you can only withdraw the gains on your investments without touching the principle. That $1 million is the golden goose; you've got to leave the goose alone and only live on the eggs if you're going to make it.

What else do you have? Yeah, Social Security might be there for us baby boomers and *maybe* Gen X, but how about you, Mr. and Mrs. Millennial? There's a good chance Social Security could adjust, amend, or go away altogether.

If you're starting to sweat a bit, I don't blame you. This is such a frustrating place to be. You thought you were doing the right things! After all, you're a millionaire! You followed the traditional planning models touted by the traditional planners, financial entertainers, and the Internet, yet you've set yourself and your spouse for a possible disaster in retirement. "Why didn't they tell me!"

I use the term *stress test* a lot when working with clients. Well, it's time for you to stress-test your plan and let's see if it works. If it doesn't, and if it's not too late, we can do something about it.

Many years ago, during the "raging eighties and nineties," when getting 15–20 percent annual returns was as simple as walking across the street, Fidelity polled their mutual fund clients. These people weren't working with a financial advisor then because, back in the day, Fidelity offered only no-load mutual funds and, as we often joked, *no-load means no advice!*

The question Fidelity asked was, "What percentage of your retirement account will you withdraw in retirement?" The most common answer was an astounding 10 percent per year. The returns of the day made that (mostly) possible.

That was then. This is now.

My industry used to use 5 percent as a reasonable annual withdrawal rate; now, it's closer to 4 percent. Due to market conditions and the longevity of Americans, many advisors are starting to suggest we might need to cut it down to 3.5 percent.

Back to our example: For purposes of this scenario, I'm focusing strictly on your retirement savings and not including your Social Security benefits. You've got $1 million and you're retiring at sixty-five. In order to avoid running out of money and avoid the risks we've identified—and leave a legacy of love to your family and/or community—you decide to take the conservative route and live on 3.5 percent of your retirement savings. That leaves you with an income of $35,000 per year, or $2,917 per month. That's right: you're a millionaire who's forced to live on $35,000.

Whenever I break this down for clients, their immediate reaction is generally:

1. Is he right?
2. Can I prove him wrong?
3. Is there something I should have done differently this whole time?

The answers are *yes, no,* and *yes*—in that order. I hate having to have this discussion with clients. There's nothing more frustrating for a financial advisor than sitting with a stressed-out couple you know you could have put on a different, more successful path if only you had been there twenty years earlier.

If you're reading this in your twenties, thirties, or forties, trust me when I say your future self is counting on you to do things right today. If you really want to end up better than a "broke millionaire" in retirement, check out some simple actions you can take today based on what we've discussed so far in this book.

Start by going back and reviewing the life insurance strategies I unpacked in chapter 8. I talked about owning term insurance from a company with the ability to convert it down the road to a cash value policy. The death benefit should be enough to replace your income, which protects your family from the loss of your income during your working years. But now, maybe ten or fifteen years from retirement, you realize your retirement income is in danger. What can you do?

The first thing you must do is save. And then save. And then save, save, and save some more. What is the last thing you're going to do? You're going to die—possibly after a long (and expensive) illness.

Well, that all sounds bleak, doesn't it? But what if we tweaked a few things before you got into that situation? Let's say at age fifty, we found the available money to convert a part of that term policy into a permanent cash value building policy. Maybe we could add a long-term care rider to it so that we've protected you against the need for care without burning through retirement funds. We fund a policy for a period of years so that it is self-sustaining and no additional money would be required to pay into it, and we would also give you the underwriting class you earned when you bought that term policy many years ago. That's what conversion is all about!

This strategy, which we planned for way in advance of retirement, would be designed for three things: long-term care for your needs while you're living; tax-free withdrawals of the cash value to enjoy, spend, and maybe do the things you never got to do; and most importantly, a tax-free legacy of love. How is life insurance tax-free, you ask? Well, death benefits to your beneficiaries are 100 percent income tax–free. If we execute the long-term care rider on your permanent life policy, all we are really doing is turning the death benefit into a living benefit for current needs. It does reduce the amount of the death benefit, but, at this time, what is more important: having access to those dollars today tax-free for your care, or preserving them for your heirs after you're gone?

Remember when I borrowed money from my life insurance policy to buy my house? That loan was 100 percent income tax–free! It never showed up on my tax return because it was a loan. Could I use that cash value tax-free later down the road for some financial need, like taking a trip around the world? Absolutely!

Some financial entertainers say permanent life insurance is a terrible decision, that it's unnecessary, that you should "buy term insurance and invest the difference"—all the objections we reviewed in the Moats section of the book. And, to be fair, that strategy works pretty well during the Accumulation and Preservation phases of your life. However, it can fall short when you are looking at Distribution and Legacy.

Now that we've taken care of your legacy, do we still need to adhere to that 3.5 percent withdrawal rate? Maybe not. What does that mean for you and your spouse? Maybe you can afford to enjoy more income in retirement. Maybe do things you didn't think you could afford to do on that 3.5 percent rate. Maybe things like:

- Help pay for your grandkids' school and college tuitions.
- Give more money away to charities.
- Travel more.
- Enjoy some luxuries you could never afford during your working years.

The list goes on and on, all because you took the initiative to educate yourself, question the financial fiction you've always taken for granted, and create unbelievable new options and opportunities for yourself!

CHAPTER 31

In Conclusion

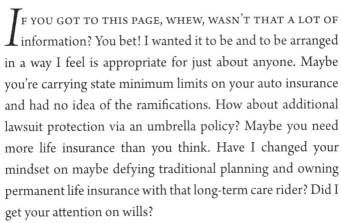

*I*F YOU GOT TO THIS PAGE, WHEW, WASN'T THAT A LOT OF information? You bet! I wanted it to be and to be arranged in a way I feel is appropriate for just about anyone. Maybe you're carrying state minimum limits on your auto insurance and had no idea of the ramifications. How about additional lawsuit protection via an umbrella policy? Maybe you need more life insurance than you think. Have I changed your mindset on maybe defying traditional planning and owning permanent life insurance with that long-term care rider? Did I get your attention on wills?

How about putting retirement planning back in a more practical position and starting to organize your cash flow with budgeting tools? Maybe open a savings account and systematically start funding it? Did you pick all your employee benefits correctly and appropriately? It may be a good time to relook at everything. Hopefully, I got your attention with the farmer paying taxes on the seed rather than the harvest. There are very few "tax-free strategies" available to you, so you should optimize what's available. Maybe you didn't know some of the investment options available to you, and I truly only scratched the surface there! Did you know that you could have many different financial buckets to create your retirement income strategy, either now or down the road as you look toward that retirement that the television ads show you?

The purpose of this book is to share multiple decades of experience in working with my clients in every area I've covered. I hope you got something from it. Now, go forth, create your own action plan, and have a wonderful life!

APPENDIX

PUTTING IT ALL TOGETHER

Simple "To-Dos" Depending

on Where You Are in Life

As I mentioned in the introduction, I find myself telling many of the same stories and having the same conversations with my prospects and clients. In lieu of reading every chapter, I've put together some simple lists for a variety of life scenarios. These are simple and easy to follow, and if you have a thought or question, you can look back to the text to get more information. If you've got ideas I can use for the next edition, please contact me at brian@briancarden.com.

WHAT TO DO IF YOU'RE JUST GETTING STARTED . . . OR STARTING OVER

The first thing to do is get off your parent's insurance plans, as you no longer live in their household and it's time to be your own person. Then . . .

Step 1: Auto Insurance

Make sure you have adequate limits so you can purchase a $1 million umbrella policy. Depending on the age of your vehicle, you might waive collision coverage, but always add comprehensive. It covers weather, theft, and flood. Include windshield repair or replacement with no deductible if your company offers it. Also add towing or roadside coverage and a rental car if needed.

Step 2: Property Insurance

Make sure your personal property is insured to full replacement. If you're renting, also add "loss of use" coverage. If the building is damaged due to fire, wind, or so on, and you cannot live there during repairs, this coverage pays you for a place to live. When a tornado recently tore through Nashville, many of my clients utilized this. Utilize that "bundle discount" that is advertised so often.

Step 3: Get a Will!

No matter your net worth or age, you need to have a contingency plan written in the event you either become incapacitated or die. We're not promised tomorrow.

Step 4: Choose a Benefits Package

If your employer offers a benefits package, review your options with a financial advisor and choose the best plan for you. Remember, these plans only cover you while employed at the company. Whatever they offer you with no additional cost, take it. Most common options are short- and long-term disability and life insurance (usually 1–2 times your salary).

Step 5: Set a Budget

Get a system for budgeting your inflows and expenses. The more you can monitor this, the less stressed you will be and the more financial margin you can create.

Step 6: Start a Monthly Savings Discipline

Even a small amount will help you get started. Open a savings account where you bank and have money systematically deposited into your account. At some point, you are going to either have a financial need for this account, or perhaps you're saving for your first home. Do it!

Step 6: Establish a 401(k)

If you're going to participate in your company 401(k) plan, max the match and no more. Choose a more aggressive fund as you're young, and this account is for the long term. If there's a Roth 401(k) option, choose that as withdrawals later in life will be 100 percent tax-free. Be aware of "auto-enrollment," as many companies will start you in the plan without you even knowing it!

WHAT TO DO WHEN YOU MOVE TO A NEW CITY OR RELOCATE WITH A JOB

Jimmy Buffett said it best: "Changes in latitudes, changes in attitudes."[35] Think about your new "want list" and write it down. Be patient, and don't rush into any decisions you might come to regret later on. Get to the new city and find a place to live—even if it's temporary. You're going to be stressed enough with the new job, new people, and new culture. If a priority is immediately buying a new home, seek out a competent real estate professional and mortgage lender. Ask your coworkers for referrals and introductions. Learn the new city. Find out what part of town works best for you, whether it's a downtown condo or a home in the suburbs.

Regarding your home/auto/umbrella insurance plans, you should look to get referrals as well. Chances are your current agent is not licensed in your new state. Don't just transfer your policies with the same company. A new relationship with an insurance advisor gives you the opportunity for a brand-new review of your coverages. Maybe a recommendation might come from that new advisor that your former advisor/agent never mentioned!

Same goes for a financial advisor. Get referrals. Find someone you like. See if their belief system aligns with yours. Remember, if you are changing companies, make sure to get those 401(k) dollars transferred to an IRA. Same goes for any company stock you might have received.

WHAT TO DO WHEN YOU GET MARRIED

The following steps are from an article I wrote for the *Nashville Business Journal* a while back. I've learned that for the younger generation, it's easier to say "I do" than to create a joint checking account.

Step One

Make sure each of you have done everything on the "Just Getting Started" appendix piece!

Step Two

If you now own a nice engagement ring, get it appraised first, then insured and added to your homeowner's policy. That way, it's insured to the full appraised value and for all risks.

Step Three

Now that you are married, you qualify for a multicar discount, so you should combine your auto insurance policies. Also make sure any renters', condo, or home policies are updated so that all personal property is included.

Step Four

Establish a joint checking account. Here's where it gets hard. Do everything you can to pay all your monthly expenses out of one checking account. Remember, it's all about optimizing every dollar, and separate accounts will not do this.

Step Five

Make beneficiary changes by adding your spouse as your beneficiary to all life insurance and company retirement plans. By law, your spouse becomes your primary beneficiary on your 401(k) plan unless they sign a form opting out.

Step Six

Agree upon financial goals and hold each other accountable to them. Write them down and keep them where you both can see them. First home, vacation, new car, entertainment, and so on. Usually one is a spender, the other a saver. Get on the same page!

Step Seven

Pay your bills *together*. This is a suggestion from personal experience. That way, you both will know what is coming in and going out. In the old days, I'd say one of you fills out the check and the other signs it, but those days are long gone.

Step Eight

Draft and execute your wills and advance directives. What if the title for the house is in one spouse's name only and they die? Could be a probate nightmare. Make sure your assets and finances are protected for your partner with a will.

WHAT TO DO IF YOU ARE SELF-EMPLOYED

I work with a lot of entrepreneurs and self-employed people. You need a good team around you.

Step One

The most important team member is a good commercial insurance broker. You will need a package policy that protects you and your business. Business insurance is totally different from your personal coverage.

Step Two

Review all of your life and disability income plans and find out where the shortfalls and gaps lie. Also make sure your savings, retirement plans, and other investments are as consolidated as possible. Don't do this alone; hire a competent advisor.

Step Three

Interview and hire a good CPA that you can grow old with. I've worked with my CPA for more than thirty years! A good CPA knows the tax code and can help you optimize your revenues and expenses. I prefer smaller boutique firms, as you can develop more of a personal relationship.

Step Four

Ask your CPA to also introduce you to potential banking relationships and maybe even legal relationships. It's important that your team is on the same page. Great personal bankers are much harder to find than in the past, but they are out there.

Step Five

Medical insurance is a must, but it can be a challenge. If you can purchase an individual plan at a reasonable cost, go there. If you're married, look to go on your spouse's plan. There are a variety of options available to you.

Step Six

Avoid putting dollars into a qualified retirement plan for the time being. One of the biggest challenges I face with my self-employed clients is overcoming their bias toward tax-deferred options. They are used to hearing, "If you put X dollars into a retirement plan, you will save Y in taxes." Yeah, but you locked those dollars away for a time later in life. What happens if you need access to it now? Remember, you should be able to "use, enjoy, and control" every dollar you can. Go back and read chapter 22 on tax deferral versus tax-free investing.

Step Seven
Surround yourself with like-minded people. Create your own mastermind group. They can be invaluable. When you're struggling or frustrated, do you really want to take that home with you?

WHAT TO DO IF YOU GET DIVORCED

Yes, I have to cover this subject, as I get several referrals a year regarding couples getting divorced. Most of the post-divorce calls I get are from women, and in many cases, they didn't control their household finances.

Hopefully, a divorce is peaceful and amicable, but we know that isn't always the case. I've seen divorces go on for years, and there's no telling how much was spent in legal fees arguing over assets, property, and, especially, children.

Step One
Hire a competent divorce attorney. Don't try to do this on your own. Let them negotiate for you. Find out exactly what they are going to do for you. In most cases, assets must be divided 50/50. It's possible that the largest assets are the most illiquid (home, business, land). These are obviously the biggest challenges.

Retirement plans are somewhat easier because they can be divided fairly easily. You are entitled to 50 percent of all contributions made and earnings received from the date of marriage to the date of divorce. Be sure to talk with your attorney about a QDRO, or "Qualified Domestic Relations Order." This is the documentation you must have for the other spouse's 401(k) plan to help divide the assets legally and fairly.

Step Two

If you're on the receiving end of a divorce, you will want a financial advisor to help you establish the right accounts to accommodate those dollars. Hire your own set of advisors! Don't rely on those that your ex-spouse has used. Go back to the first section on getting started, because that's exactly what you're doing!

WHAT TO DO IF YOU ARE 50+ AND AREN'T AS PREPARED FOR RETIREMENT AS YOU HOPED

Yes, I see this quite frequently. Remember what John Lennon said? "Life is what happens to you while you're busy making other plans."[36]

Let's return to the question we explored in chapter 28: Which would you prefer? A big pile of money at retirement age, or a lifetime income you and your spouse cannot outlive? Think carefully. If you chose the latter, then I think we have a higher chance of success.

The days of hitting Social Security age and getting a pension are gone. Most of us will work later in life . . . either because we want to, or because we have to!

Traditional planning says to max the 401(k) and save as much as you can . . . while paying the house off and putting the kids through college. You can easily see how much financial stress you're putting on yourself. Hire a competent financial advisor who focuses more on the plan and the outcome than a product sale. Stop thinking about retirement and build a plan that will not only get you there, but will have some assurances as well for you and your spouse. Now is the time to not only reach but exceed "world-class savings habits."

Remember that one of your greatest risks at this point in your lives is living too long! Longevity risk poses one of the greatest challenges.

WHAT TO DO IF YOU'RE IN RETIREMENT

What goes around, comes around. The first thing is to make sure you've done all the tasks as if you're "getting started," but now you've got to add some things.

Step One
Plan ahead for any long-term care needs. There's a 70 percent chance of needing some form of care in your retirement years.

Step Two

Make sure your wills, trusts, and powers of attorney are completed in full with contingents in place. Now is the time to make your wishes known *in writing*. If you have adult children, share these documents with them so they know what you and/or your spouse want as you age. We've all heard the horror stories of a parent or grandparent dying with no will and the issues created by that. Don't be that person.

Step Three

Find a good Medicare advisor. Medicare planning is its own animal and it's one product I do not sell, so I won't give advice here other than to find a competent professional who specializes in these coverages. Find them and hire them!

Step Four

Set a new budget. What day of the week do you and your spouse spend the most money? Probably the weekend days, right? Now that you're retired, every day is a weekend day! Depending on your plan and your monthly budget, hopefully you have built in some margin for those extra things, whatever they might be.

Step Five

Consider giving some of your legacy while you're still around to see the recipients appreciate it. I've worked with so many "Depression-era" clients who struggle emotionally to spend their assets. All they've ever known is save, save, save. I remember having lunch with one client and I told him, "You know, you're in good financial shape. Which would you prefer—them receiving an inheritance from you after you're gone, or you giving them a gift now and seeing their appreciation yourself?"

He looked at me with a big, bright smile and said, "You know, I never thought of that! I would *love* to share in their joy and see their excitement!"

He went home and started setting up meetings with his family members. He told me later those meetings were some of the most fun he's ever had.

NOTES

1. Talk with your CPA for more details.
2. Brad Schrade and Brian Haas, "Record-breaking Flood Displaces Thousands in Middle Tenn.," *The Tennessean* (Nashville), May 3, 2010, ProQuest.
3. Brad Schrade and Anne Paine, "In-depth Report: Army Corps of Engineers Struggled with Dams, Forecasts," *The Tennessean* (Nashville), May 9, 2010, ProQuest.
4. "Remembering the May 2010 Flood," National Weather Service, accessed September 21, 2021, https://www.weather.gov/ohx/may2010flood.
5. Nate Rau, "Flood Damage Tops $1.9 Billion," *The Tennessean* (Nashville), May 20, 2010, ProQuest.
6. Some companies actually call it a *Long-Term Care rider*, while others use the terminology of *Chronic Illness rider*. For purposes of this writing, there are some differences, but not a lot.
7. Lorrie Konish, "This Is the Real Reason Most Americans File for Bankruptcy," CNBC.com, February 11, 2019, https://www.cnbc.com/2019/02/11/this-is-the-real-reason-most-americans-file-for-bankruptcy.html.
8. For the purposes of this chapter, and because I am not a lawyer, I'm keeping the discussion on a very high level. One of my estate planning attorneys, Matthew Mullins, JD, has also helped with the drafting of the subject manner.
9. "Personal Saving Rate," Federal Reserve Economic Data (FRED), Federal Reserve Bank of St. Louis, last updated June 25, 2021, https://fred.stlouisfed.org/data/PSAVERT.txt.
10. U.S. Bureau of Labor Statistics, "Employee Tenure in 2020," news release no. USDL-20-1791, September 22, 2020, https://www.bls.gov/news.release/archives/tenure_09222020.htm.
11. "Effective Federal Funds Rate (FEDFUNDS)," Federal Reserve Economic Data (FRED), Federal Reserve Bank of St. Louis, last updated September 1, 2021, https://fred.stlouisfed.org/series/FEDFUNDS.

12 Disclosure: This is intended for illustrative purposes only and should not be construed as advice. Consult your advisor regarding your personal situation.

13 "HSA IRS Guidelines, Contribution Limits, and Eligible Expenses," HSA Bank, accessed September 22, 2021, https://www.hsabank.com/hsabank/learning-center/irs-contribution-limits-and-guidelines.

14 Anna Helhoski and Ryan Lane, "Student Loan Debt Statistics: 2021," Nerd-Wallet, last updated August 9, 2021, https://www.nerdwallet.com/article/loans/student-loans/student-loan-debt#average-student-loan-debt.

15 "Retirement Topics—401(k) and Profit-Sharing Plan Contribution Limits," Internal Revenue Service, accessed September 23, 2021, https://www.irs.gov/retirement-plans/plan-participant-employee/retirement-topics-401k-and-profit-sharing-plan-contribution-limits.

16 "History of the U.S. Marginal Tax Rates 1913–2009," Ouida Vincent, March 26, 2010, http://ouidavincent.com/wp-content/uploads/2010/03/History-of-US-Marginal-Tax-Rates3.pdf.

17 Gary P. Brinson, Brian D. Singer, and Gilbert L. Beebower, "Determinants of Portfolio Performance II: An Update," *Financial Analysts Journal* 47, no. 3 (1991): 40–48, https://www.jstor.org/stable/4479432. Disclosure: Asset allocation or diversification does not ensure a profit or guarantee against loss; it is a method used to manage investment risk.

18 Steve Vernon, "Living Too Long Is a Risk!," CBS News, July 24, 2013, https://www.cbsnews.com/news/living-too-long-is-a-risk/.

19 Julia Kagan, "Fiduciary," Investopedia, April 6, 2021, https://www.investopedia.com/terms/f/fiduciary.asp#:~:text=A%20fiduciary%20is%20a%20person,preserve%20good%20faith%20and%20trust.

20 Disclosure: This is intended for illustrative purposes only and should not be construed as advice.

21 Disclosure: This is intended for illustrative purposes only and should not be construed as advice. Your results may vary.

22 BrokerCheck by FINRA is available online at www.finra.org/brokercheck.

23 Will Kenton, "S&P 500 Index—Standard & Poor's 500 Index," Investopedia, last modified March 22, 2021, https://www.investopedia.com/terms/s/sp500.asp.

24 *The Man Who Shot Liberty Valance*, directed by John Ford, starring James Stewart, John Wayne, and Vera Miles (1962; Hollywood, CA: Paramount,

2001), DVD.

25 DALBAR, Inc., *Quantitative Analysis of Investor Behavior,* 2020, https://wealthwatchadvisors.com/wp-content/uploads/2020/03/QAIB_PremiumEdition2020_WWA.pdf.

26 Gary P. Brinson, Brian D. Singer, and Gilbert L. Beebower, "Determinants of Portfolio Performance II: An Update," *Financial Analysts Journal* 47, no. 3 (1991): 40–48, https://www.jstor.org/stable/4479432.

27 Lauren Perez, "Average U.S. Savings Account Balance 2021: A Demographic Breakdown," ValuePenguin, accessed September 25, 2021, https://www.valuepenguin.com/banking/average-savings-account-balance.

28 "What's the Median Retirement Savings by Age?," Synchrony Bank, November 10, 2020, https://www.synchronybank.com/blog/median-retirement-savings-by-age/.

29 You can find your personal Social Security benefit statements online at www.ssa.gov.

30 Robert C. Merton, "The Crisis in Retirement Planning," *Harvard Business Review,* July/August 2014, 3, https://robertcmerton.com/wp-content/uploads/2017/08/The-Crisis-in-Retirement-Planning-HBR-2014-Merton.pdf.

31 *The Shawshank Redemption,* directed by Frank Darabont, starring Tim Robbins and Morgan Freeman (1994; Beverly Hills, CA: Castle Rock Entertainment, 1999), DVD.

32 Disclosure: I am not a licensed Realtor, nor will I ever be. However, I do understand the strategies they offer as investment vehicles, and I have had this very conversation with myriad licensed agents.

33 Benjamin Harris, "Why Older Couples Must Look Beyond Life Expectancy When Planning for Retirement," *The Wall Street Journal* online, last modified February 5, 2019, https://www.wsj.com/articles/why-older-couples-must-look-beyond-life-expectancy-when-planning-for-retirement-01549380699.

34 John Lennon, "Beautiful Boy (Darling Boy)," track 7 on *Double Fantasy,* Geffen Records, 1980.

35 Jimmy Buffett, "Changes in Latitudes, Changes in Attitudes," track 1 on *Changes in Latitudes, Changes in Attitudes,* ABC Records, 1977.

36 John Lennon, "Beautiful Boy (Darling Boy)," track 7 on *Double Fantasy,* Geffen Records, 1980.